IRELAND FOR TOURISTS

The Traveler's Guide to Make The Most Out of Your Trip to Ireland - *Where to Go, Eat,* Sleep & Party

By Dagny Taggart

Disclaimer

The information provided in this book is designed to provide helpful information on the subjects discussed. The author's books are only meant to provide the reader with the basics travel guidelines of a certain location, without any warranties regarding the accuracy of the information and advice provided. Each traveler should do their own research before departing

Table of Contents

MY FREE GIFT TO YOU! 7

LEARN ANY LANGUAGE 300% FASTER 8

INTRODUCTION: WHY YOU WILL FALL IN LOVE WITH IRELAND 9

PART I: PLANNING YOUR TRIP AHEAD (TIPS, BUDGET & THINGS YOU MUST KNOW) 10

AN OVERVIEW OF IRELAND'S REGIONS AND COUNTIES 11
GETTING ALONG WITH THE IRISH 11
WHAT TO EAT IN IRELAND 14
HEALTH, SAFETY, AND PRACTICAL CONCERNS 15
BUDGETING 17
GETTING AROUND 18

PART II: LEINSTER (THE EAST) 21

DUBLIN 21
WHERE TO STAY 21
GETTING IN AND GETTING AROUND 22
KEY SIGHTS IN DUBLIN 25
HISTORY NOTE: 30
THE EASTER RISING AND THE WAR OF INDEPENDENCE 30
EATING IN DUBLIN 32
PUBS & CLUBS 33
TEMPLE BAR DISTRICT 35
FESTIVALS IN DUBLIN 36
CULTURE NOTE: 37
ST. PATRICK'S, SHAMROCKS, AND THE "LUCK OF THE IRISH" 37
OUTSIDE DUBLIN 39

PART III: CONNACHT 42

GETTING INTO CONNACHT 42

GALWAY 44

GETTING AROUND IN GALWAY 45

KEY SIGHTS IN GALWAY 45

WHERE TO STAY 47

WHERE TO EAT 48

PUBS & CLUBS 49

GETTING OUT OF GALWAY: THE CONNEMARA COUNTRYSIDE 50

THE ARAN ISLANDS 52

THE BURREN AND THE CLIFFS OF MOHER 54

CULTURE NOTE: THE IRISH LANGUAGE 58

SLIGO 59

PART IV: MUNSTER (THE SOUTH) 63

CORK 64

HISTORY NOTE: 70

THE GREAT FAMINE 70

KILLARNEY 71

THE RING OF KERRY 73

THE DINGLE PENINSULA 76

PART V: ULSTER (THE NORTH) 80

HISTORY NOTE: 81

UNDERSTANDING THE TROUBLES 81

BELFAST 82

WHERE TO STAY 84

EATING IN BELFAST 84

PUBS & CLUBS 85

CULTURE NOTE: 91

THE HOUND OF ULSTER 91

DONEGAL 93

PART VI: NO ONE LEAVES IRELAND FOR LONG 96

LEARN ANY LANGUAGE 300% FASTER 98

PS: CAN I ASK YOU A QUICK FAVOR? 99

PREVIEW OF "ENGLAND FOR TOURISTS - THE TRAVELER'S TRAVEL GUIDE TO MAKE THE MOST OUT OF YOUR TRIP TO ENGLAND - WHERE TO GO, EAT, SLEEP & PARTY" 100

CHECK OUT MY OTHER BOOKS 109

ABOUT THE AUTHOR 110

Dedicated to those who love going beyond their own frontiers.

Keep on traveling,

Dagny Taggart

My FREE Gift to You!

As a way of saying thank you for downloading my book, I'd like to send you an exclusive gift that will revolutionize the way you learn new languages. It's an extremely comprehensive PDF with 15 language hacking rules that **will help you learn 300% <u>faster</u>, with <u>less effort</u>, and with <u>higher than ever retention rates</u>**.

This guide is an amazing complement to the book you just got, and could easily be a stand-alone product, but for now I've decided to give it away for free, to thank you for being such an awesome reader, and to make sure I give you all the value that I can to help you succeed faster on your language learning journey.

To get your FREE gift, click on the link or the button below, follow the steps, and I'll send it to your email address right away.

>> <u>http://bitly.com/Language-Gift</u> <<

GET INSTANT ACCESS

Learn Any Language 300% FASTER

>> Get Full Online Language Courses With Audio Lessons <<

Would you like to learn a new language before you start your trip? I think that's a great idea. Now, why don't you do it 300% *FASTER*?

I've partnered with the most revolutionary language teachers to bring you the very language online courses I've ever seen. It's a mind-blowing program specifically created for language hackers such as ourselves. It will allow you learn ANY language, from French to Chinese, 3x faster, straight from the comfort of your own home, office, or wherever you may be. It's like having an unfair advantage!

You can choose from a wide variety of languages, such as French, Spanish, Italian, German, Chinese, Portuguese, and A TON more.

Each Online Course consists of:

+ 91 Built-In Lessons
+ 33 Interactive Audio Lessons
+ 24/7 Support to Keep You Going

The program is extremely engaging, fun, and easy-going. You won't even notice you are learning a complex foreign language from scratch. And before you realize it, by the time you go through all the lessons you will officially become a truly solid speaker.

Old classrooms are a thing of the past. It's time for a revolution.

If you'd like to go the extra mile, then follow the link below, and let the revolution begin!

>> http://bitly.com/foreign-language-courses <<

CHECK OUT THE COURSE »

Introduction
Why You Will Fall In Love With Ireland

When the Romans under Julius Caesar first began their conquest of Great Britain, they looked to the west and saw the dim outlines of another land. From travelers' tales, they knew it was inhabited by human beings, but they knew nothing about this mysterious tribe or their territory. They believed the island to be hostile in climate, poor in natural resources, and hardly worth conquering. On their maps, they labeled it "Hibernia" after their word *hibernus*, meaning "wintry."

How little those Roman conquerors knew. Because they decided not to cross those 60 miles of choppy water, the small island's Celtic inhabitants were allowed to continue developing their culture for thousands of years without the interference of a colonial master.

Today, that mysterious island bears the proud name of Ireland, a name that inspires love, joy, and intense loyalty all over the world – and not just among the Irish and their descendants! As the worldwide popularity of St. Patrick's day shows, there's something universally recognizable about Irish culture. Something in its combination of rich history, joyous music, and irrepressible humor seems to appeal to the depths of every human soul.

What is it that makes this island so magical?

The only way to understand it is to walk Ireland's hills and forests; to spend time talking with its inhabitants; and to see, taste, touch, and smell the richness of this inimitable corner of the world.

This book is a guide to doing exactly that. I want to help you *know* Ireland, not just visit it. If you can experience it properly, this island will enchant you just as it has enchanted thousands of other travelers over the centuries.

Sláinte.

Enjoy!

Part I
Planning Your Trip Ahead (Tips, Budget & Things You Must Know)

(image courtesy of Wikimedia Commons)

Ireland (like this book) is divided into four sections, or provinces: Leinster, Connacht, Munster, and Ulster. Each of these provinces was once a separate kingdom, but today they have very little political significance. The most important unit of human geography today is the *county*. Irish people strongly identify with their county, and each one has its own personality, accent, and cultural heritage.

Leinster (the East)

Historically, Leinster was thought of as the most wealthy and profitable of the kingdoms, largely because of its huge trading port: Dublin. Dublin still dominates the scene in Leinster, but there are other sites to be seen as well once you get out of the city.

Connacht (the West)

Thought to be the home of Ireland's most powerful druids and enchanters, Connacht still casts its inescapable spell on travelers. Connacht is home to some of the most dramatic landscapes on the island, and its main city – Galway – is considered Ireland's cultural capital.

Munster (the South)

Ancient Celtic epics tell of great bards, singers and poets emerging from the rustic landscapes of southern Ireland. This is still true today, as the southern counties of Cork and Kerry produce some of Ireland's finest music, and are the best place to hear Irish (Gaelic) spoken as an everyday language.

Ulster (the North)

The historic kingdom of Ulster includes not only Northern Ireland (part of the U.K.), but also three counties in the Republic of Ireland. In ancient times, long before Northern Ireland was separated from the rest of the island, Ulster was home to Ireland's most fearsome warriors.

Getting Along with the Irish

Here's a little advice on Irish etiquette: don't be a jerk. That's pretty much all you need to know.

The Irish are famously easygoing, and welcome strangers very readily. Best of all, they tend to be pretty straight shooters – if you do something rude, someone will gently let you know and set you straight with a smile.

Here, though, are a few missteps to avoid while you're in the country:

1. **Respect people's property,** especially when it comes to fences and gates.

Walking in the countryside is one of the most glorious experiences Ireland has to offer, and the locals are well aware of it. (Tell anyone in the western counties you're going for a "hill walk" and they'll probably pepper you with advice on the best routes and vistas.) But unlike in the U.S., most of your hiking will be on private property rather than public land, and more often than not you'll be trekking right through someone's back yard. So be respectful! Be sure to say hello if you run into the owner, and if you open a gate to pass through, always ALWAYS close it behind you.

2. **Joke around – respectfully.**

The Irish are rightly renowned for their sense of humor, which ranges from dry and biting to bawdy and raucous. Strangers are often welcomed with jokes and maybe a little good-natured teasing, and you should feel free to crack a few jokes in response. But certain topics – especially race and religion – are not considered appropriate for humor. The Irish have suffered truly calamitous violence over the past several centuries, and much of it has been ethnically or religiously motivated. You could well be talking to someone who lost a friend or relative in the Troubles. Similarly, many people will be offended if you joke about the Great Potato Famine or the Catholic Laws that oppressed the Irish people under British rule. In some cases, the Irish are also sensitive about their reputation as a heavy-drinking culture. The majority find this stereotype humorous (and perhaps see a little truth in it), but some people have been hurt by alcoholism and may not appreciate your making light of it. Just be careful.

3. **Know what country you're in**

Northern Ireland (dark) and the Republic of Ireland (light yellow)

This should be obvious. But you'd be surprised how many travelers move between the Republic of Ireland and the U.K. without realizing that they've changed countries. It's pretty simple, though: the northeast corner of the island is Northern Ireland. They are part of the United Kingdom and use the Pound. The rest of the island is the Republic of Ireland, which is an independent country and is on the Euro. It was not even a hundred years ago that this part of Ireland fought a bloody war to win their independence from the U.K., and they will not soon forget the differences between themselves and the British – you shouldn't either. (Similarly, don't confuse the Irish with their distant Celtic cousins, the Scottish.)

4. <u>Tip modestly, but not TOO modestly</u>

Tipping is a relatively new phenomenon in Ireland, where barkeeps and waiters were normally paid a living wage – they didn't live on tips the way service workers often do in America. However, this is changing and it's now customary to tip those who serve your food and drinks, especially in more heavily touristed areas like Dublin and Belfast. 10-15% for good service is usually fine.

5. <u>Think before you drink</u>

The Irish love a good time, but they also expect everyone to know their limits and never drink to excess. If you find yourself vomiting, invading people's personal space, or acting inappropriately, your drunkenness will not be seen as an excuse, and certainly won't be viewed as cute or funny. You'll just embarrass yourself and irritate the locals. Be smart!

Also, there are a couple of drinks you simply shouldn't order in Ireland. One, for obvious reasons, is the Irish Car Bomb. This refers to the violence in Northern Ireland, and is a form of dark humor that will not go over well with your bartender. Also, the Black-and-Tan is a popular beer-based cocktail with a seemingly innocuous name. However, it's named after the so-called "Black and Tan Squads," the brutally violent enforcers who were sent to suppress dissent in Ireland during the War of Independence. Most Irish people are sufficiently aware of their history to know this reference, and you don't want to appear ignorant or insensitive.

What to Eat in Ireland

It's less a matter of *what* you eat in Ireland than of *how much*. Everywhere you go, someone will be looking to load up your plate with something hot and filling. Ireland isn't exactly renowned for its cuisine, but what it lacks in culinary variety it more than makes up for in quality and heartiness. The specialty dish is **Irish stew**, an aromatic blend of potatoes, root vegetables, seasoning, and a healthy dose of beef or lamb. You'll find that the Irish can make almost anything with potatoes (and very rarely make anything *without* potatoes). They also love to add **Guinness** to their cooking. Guinness pie, Guinness cake, Guinness stew – it's hard to go wrong, honestly.

The Irish will also whip up global favorites like pasta, hamburgers, and sandwiches. And they usually do an excellent job of it – if you're ever in Ballydavid and you find yourself in a corner booth at T.P.'s Pub, make sure you get a bowl of his spaghetti with meat sauce. Tell him I sent you.

It's well known that the Irish get more pleasure out of their beverages than their food. Here, the Irish specialties fall into two categories: whiskey and beer. **Irish whiskey** has a clean, understated flavor – similar to Scotch, though a little less earthy. The American whiskey connoisseur, accustomed to bourbons and Tennessee sour mash whiskeys, may find it a little odd at first, but there's a whole world of Irish whiskeys to explore, and those who make and drink it are more than happy to make recommendations. (Beware, though! In whiskey as in everything else, it's never a good idea to confuse Irish with Scottish).

Irish beer has a far more global following than their whiskey. If you know nothing else about Ireland's exports, you probably know about one thing: Guinness Stout. What you may not realize is that you've probably never had it. The beer that Americans call "Guinness" is actually brewed in Toronto, not Ireland, and it has a very different flavor from real Irish Guinness! One tip: when you're served a Guinness, the barkeep will set it aside for several minutes to let it settle and breathe. Like decanting a fine wine, this is considered an indispensable part of the process of serving Guinness stout, and should not be skipped. Be patient!

Health, Safety, and Practical Concerns

EMERGENCY NUMBER: 999 or 112

Safety is a pleasantly straightforward topic in Ireland. Be smart. But don't worry.

Crime

Crime is a relatively minor issue in Ireland, though you should expect roughly what you'd expect anywhere else in Europe – things get a little worse in the bigger cities, and you need to be careful with your valuables. But people frequently leave their doors unlocked in the countryside, and there's very little violent crime. Most police officers don't even carry guns.

Northern Ireland, especially Belfast, has a reputation as being violent and even war-torn – we'll explore the history of that violence in Part V, but for now it's enough to say that travelers have nothing to worry about. Ever since the peace agreement in 1998, the incidence of terrorist attacks has declined dramatically, and although the political situation remains tense, there are no signs of an immanent eruption of violence.

The police in Ireland are known as the *Gardaí* (sing. *Garda*), often simply called the "guards." They're extremely courteous and helpful, and quite happy to assist tourists.

Traffic

Drive on the left in Ireland. Better yet, don't drive at all, especially in the countryside. These days, the roads are generally well-maintained and drivers obey the laws, but this is a relatively new development. Before the influx of EU money, the Irish countryside had a notoriously unreliable infrastructure, and cars would frequently drive right down the centerline rather than staying in their lane. This has led to hair-raising stories, still passed down in many youth hostels and tourist-heavy barrooms across the island. Although things have improved dramatically over the last couple of decades, it's still best to leave your driving needs in the hands of experienced locals.

Staying Healthy

Ireland has no special health concerns, but normal precautions always apply:

- Keep your shoes on when walking in rural areas.

- Watch out for drivers coming in from the left – it's surprisingly disorienting.

- Bring prescription medications with you, as some medications can be difficult to find abroad.

Because of a health scare in the mid-90s, some people are concerned that Irish beef may be contaminated with mad cow disease. This fear is unfounded, however, as the mad cow outbreak was nearly 20 years ago and there have been no indications that it is coming back. (Even when it was at its worst, the risks were fairly slight.) Besides, the Irish export about 90% of their beef production, so the risks are certainly no greater here than they would be in other parts of Europe. Enjoy as much Irish beef as you like!

If you do get sick in Ireland, you can walk into most doctor's offices and ask for a consultation, which most likely will cost under €100.

Although Ireland's healthcare system is excellent, hospitals and doctor's offices sometimes experience overcrowding, and this may delay your care somewhat. However, most Americans from major cities are unfortunately pretty accustomed to long waits at the emergency room, so the delays in Irish healthcare won't seem so bad by comparison.

The Seasons

Ireland experiences all four seasons in dramatic fashion. Often, in fact, you'll get all four of them in a single day! Situated in the middle of the turbulent North Atlantic, the island is extremely unpredictable in terms of weather, especially on the windswept western coastline. There's **no bad season to**

visit Ireland, but here's some of what you can expect depending on when you choose to go:

	Pros	Cons
Fall	Rainbows every day (literally) Festivals! Generally pleasant temperature	Frequent rainshowers High winds Occasional (very) cold days
Winter	Christmastime in Ireland Picturesque snow on the hills No crowds	Cold Very few hours of daylight Trails often closed
Spring	The Emerald Isle in bloom Festivals! Adorable baby lambs everywhere	Occasional cold days Lingering snow may close trails Not yet in full greenery
Summer	Gorgeous weather Green, green, green! Long hours of daylight	High tourist season Prices often higher

Budgeting

Prices fluctuate a fair bit in Ireland for two reasons:

1) **The Euro.** Ireland is on the Euro, which has seen some instability recently against the dollar. Things are more stable now than they were a few years ago, but the Euro still fluctuates and this will determine the price of everything on the island, from hotels and restaurants to taxis and souvenirs

2) **The Irish economy.** Again, things have improved recently, but the Irish economy was hit extremely hard by the global downturn of 2008-09. The collapse of the so-called "Celtic Tiger" caused a ruinous recession in Ireland, which created some volatility in prices.

Despite these instabilities, you can plan a trip to Ireland around pretty much any sort of budget.

Sample Budgets:

Backpacker (€35/day)	You're staying in large-occupancy rooms at the

	youth hostel and getting around primarily by bus (or foot). You generally eat modest meals or cook in the hostel kitchen, and you mind your budget when you go out drinking. Your primary activities include hiking, independent sightseeing, photography, etc.
Tourist (€100/day)	You stay in mid-range or budget hotels with your own room. You can eat at any standard restaurant, and your alcohol budget is a little looser. Your activities include theater performances, museums, and shopping, and your primary mode of transportation is a combination of busses and trains.
Jet-Setter (€200+)	You stay in the finest hotels and enjoy international cuisine at high-end restaurants. At this budget level, your options for activities and entertainment are pretty much limitless.

Key prices (approximate):

Train (Dublin-Galway)	€40
Bus (Dublin-Galway)	€25
Guinness Storehouse tour	€13.50
One night in a youth hostel	€15-25
One night in a mid-range hotel	€40-50
One night in a luxury hotel	€100+
Mid-range alcoholic beverage	€3-5
Steaming bowl of Irish stew	€7-10

Getting Around

If you're planning a trip to Ireland, you'll want to find ways to see as much of this diverse island as possible. Here are a few of the options for getting from place to place quickly and conveniently.

Rental Cars

Unless you're going to be in Ireland for an extended period of time, it's generally not worth it to rent a car. It's tough to get used to driving on the left, the traffic can be a hassle, and you have so many other options!

However, if you want complete freedom to traverse the countryside and set your own schedule, there's obviously no better method than a rental car. Just be prepared, if you're going into the rural areas, to stop for long periods behind flocks of obstinate sheep.

Taxis

Ireland has many highly experienced cab drivers who are willing to make fairly long trips. Although this is one of the more expensive ways to get around, it's a great opportunity to get an insider's views on what to do at each stop along your itinerary.

Trains

Ireland is crisscrossed by a network of extremely efficient trains, and watching the countryside fly by from the comfort of a train seat can be one of the most enjoyable parts of your trip! The one disadvantage of going by train is that nearly all the routes go through Dublin, which can be inconvenient for certain itineraries.

Buses

Fortunately, if there's no direct train route to your destination, you can always take *Bus Eireann* (pronounced "AIR-ann"), which covers even the most remote corners of the island. These buses are, of course, much slower than a train, but they follow equally picturesque routes and afford many opportunities for through-the-window photography.

Planes

For the truly time-strapped traveler, there are some domestic flights that will get you from one end of Ireland to the other very quickly. The longest flight within the island, however, is from Cork airport in the south all the way up to Belfast in Northern Ireland, a distance of just over 200 miles. So the flight might save you a couple of hours in total, but it wouldn't be much more than that, and you would miss out on all those miles of beautiful scenery out your window!

Ferries

Several spots in Ireland offer inexpensive ferries. This is a great way to visit the Aran Islands, get from the Dingle Peninsula to Iveragh Peninsula (County Kerry), or go to Wales, Scotland, or England for a day. There's also a direct ferry from Cork to Roscoff, France, but it takes significantly longer than a flight.

By Foot

If you want to get a feel for the Irish landscape, there's no better option than walking. Ireland is covered with world-class foot trails, from gently sloping coastlines to dramatic, heart-pounding mountain summits. The best places to walk/hike are Counties Cork, Kerry, Galway, Mayo, Sligo, and Donegal (more or less the whole of the western coast).

Part II
Leinster (The East)

Dublin

Raised on songs and stories, heroes of renown;
Ah, the passing tales of glory that once was Dublin town

When you say "the east" in Ireland, you're largely talking about Dublin. This vibrant city is the seat of Ireland's government and the center of its youth culture, athletics, and nightlife. With a population of 527,000, the city is home to well over 10% of Ireland's population, and it's also hands-down the most tourist-heavy part of the island.

Where to Stay

Where you stay in Dublin depends on what you're looking to get out of the city. If you're here for the nightlife, go with the Temple Bar district (see p. 20). Temple Bar has accommodations at every level, from a large youth hostel up to a number of high-end hotels. But be ready for noise! The party goes on all night in the Temple Bar, and you may have trouble getting to sleep, if sleep is really what you're interested in.

If you're more into history and culture, look around Grafton Street, just south of Temple Bar near Trinity College. Although less raucous than Temple Bar, this district is also thick with hostels and hotels, and puts you right in the center of Dublin's museums, theaters, shops, and historic sites. It's also near the **Dublin Tourism Information Centre** (Suffolk Street, Dublin 2), which is probably the best first stop for any visitor to Dublin.

Getting In and Getting Around

Dublin Airport

All flights to Dublin come in via Dublin Airport near the northern suburb of Swords. It's roughly a half-hour from the city center in light traffic, and well served by buses. The cheapest way to get into town is the Dublin Bus, which will take you into the city center for just €2.65. (You can take either route 41 or 16, depending on which part of the city you want to get to).

Train Stations

If you're arriving in Dublin via train, you'll come into one of two stations. Trains from the western counties arrive at **Heuston**, which is a couple of miles west of the city center right along the River Liffey. It's a gorgeous walk if you don't have too much luggage!

The other train station is **Connolly**, just a few blocks north of the city center. This station primarily serves trains to Belfast and other destinations in the north.

Both of these train stations have taxi queues day and night, and of course are served by the city buses. However, because central Dublin is so compact, it's often easiest just to **walk**. This way, you get the added advantage of exploring the city a little on your way to the hotel or hostel!

Busáras

Inter-city buses all arrive at Busáras Terminal, right next to the Connolly train station. Again, you'll probably be within walking distance of your destination, but if not a cab driver will be able to assist you.

Dublin is one of the most compact capitals in Europe. The majority of sightseeing destinations, historic bars, shops, and restaurants are all clustered within about a 2-mile radius of Trinity College in the center of town. This makes the city extremely walkable, and the experience of strolling along the river, taking in the music of Irish life, is one of the most pleasant aspects of any trip to Dublin.

Public transportation is available, of course, but it's generally geared more toward commuters than tourists. If you're looking to take in all of Dublin's sights within a short time, one of the best options is a **Hop-On Hop-Off Bus Tour**, which for about €20 will give you access to any of the buses that circulate through the major tourist destinations. In addition to convenient transportation, this also gives you the advantage of a professional tour guide.

There are also plenty of **taxis** in Dublin, and they're about as reliable as they would be in other European capitals. Occasionally, you'll encounter a cab driver who wants to fleece tourists by taking them on long, circuitous routes and overcharging at the end. This is uncommon, however, and is banned by the drivers' union. Should a driver attempt this con on you, get in touch with the Independent Workers' Union, Dublin Taxi Drivers' Branch.

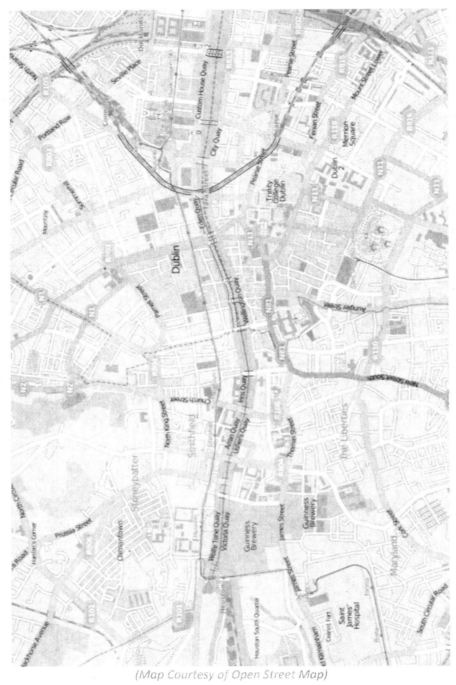

(Map Courtesy of Open Street Map)

Key Sights in Dublin

Trinity College

The Long Room at Trinity College Library
(photo credit: Superchilum via Wikimedia Commons)

Trinity College is a historic campus right in the heart of central Dublin. The campus itself is a stunning architectural specimen, an oasis of quiet study within the noise and chaos of central Dublin. Its central buildings all face a single central quad with only one main entrance, which helps to create the pervasive feeling of tranquility.

Trinity College is also home to the **Long Room**, one of the most beautiful library spaces in the world. The Long Room displays historic documents from the Irish War of Independence alongside manuscripts from the many great authors who did their work in this city of book lovers.

The prize display at Trinity College, though, is the Book of Kells, an exquisite illuminated manuscript from the 8th century AD. The book is one of the best examples of medieval Celtic art, and its interlacing designs have inspired countless imitations, from calligraphic art to tattoos.

St. Patrick's Cathedral

Since its founding in 1191, this majestic (and somewhat intimidating) cathedral has dominated the modest skyline of central Dublin. In addition to its inspiring architecture and long history, the cathedral is also notable for the statue of Benjamin Guinness – yes, *that* Guinness – the brewer and philanthropist who helped renovate the building in the 19th century.

O'Connell Street

Across the river from the Temple Bar is Dublin's *Avenue des Champs-Élysées* – O'Connell Street. This broad avenue through the city center is home to countless shops, restaurants, and pubs. It's also home to the **Spire of Dublin**, a 400-foot-tall sculpture in the shape of a giant glittering needle. The ultra-modern Spire (considered the world's tallest sculpture) occupies the former spot of Nelson's Pillar, a British statue that was blown down by a bomb in 1966, marking the symbolic beginning of The Troubles. When the Spire was erected in its place 30 years later, it was a symbol of peace overcoming violence as Ireland's past fades into its coming future.

St. Stephen's Green

For a little peace and quiet, it's hard to beat St. Stephen's Green. This large classical garden is only a couple of blocks from St. Patrick's Cathedral, and its open grassy spaces and placid water provide an unbeatable backdrop for a picnic or just an afternoon of people watching.

The World's Most Photogenic Beer
(photo by the author)

Guinness Storehouse and the Gravity Bar

The actual Guinness brewery has been moved out of the city center, but the Storehouse now houses a visitor's center and museum where you can learn all about how Ireland's favorite beer is brewed. It's a great lesson in history even if you aren't a big beer fan. But if you *are* a beer fan, this is a must. After the tour, you'll be given a free drink ticket, which you can take up to the **Gravity Bar** on the top floor. This bar offers a 360º view of Dublin, and you can sip the freshest Guinness you'll ever taste while gazing out at one of the city's finest views.

Kilmainham Gaol

Not for the faint of heart. This historic *gaol* (jail) housed revolutionaries and Catholic dissidents, and was the spot where the ringleaders of the Easter Rising (see p. 18) were executed. Its haunting interior is highly evocative of the suffering of these prisoners, and the tour guides are extremely knowledgeable about the bloody history of 20th-century Ireland.

The Four Courts at Dawn
(photo by the author)

Walking "Sweet Anna Liffey"

The River Liffey is Dublin's beating heart. The river winds slowly through the center of town and many important historic sites are located along its banks. One of the most architecturally arresting is the **Four Courts** (right), a building that was almost destroyed by artillery in 1916, but miraculously survived and now houses the Irish national court. "Sweet Anna Liffey," as the classic song calls her, is the ultimate emblem of the city's heritage.

National Museum of Ireland

Contrary to its title, this is not a single museum, but rather a collection of museums scattered around the city. They include the Museum of

Archaeology, Museum of **Decorative Arts and History**, and Museum of **Natural History**. Each is well worth a visit, depending on the particular tastes of each traveler. However, since the museums are **free**, you may as well visit all three of them!

Dublinia & the Viking World

A must-see for history buffs, and a great attraction for kids. This heritage center explores the early history of the city, starting with its founding by Viking raiders and traders around 900 AD.

Dublin Zoo

Pretty much standard fare as far as zoos go. This one is the largest in Ireland and definitely worth a trip if you're traveling with kids and want to let them see a wide variety of animals up close. It's also a respectable operation and is highly-regarded for its conservation efforts.

Molly Malone

Molly Malone with Her Cart
(photo credit: Philip Halling via Creative Commons)

"In Dublin's fair city / where the girls are so pretty / I first set my eyes on sweet Molly Malone as she wheeled her wheel-barrow / through streets broad and narrow / Crying, 'Cockles and mussels, alive, alive, oh!'"

This song, one of the most famous ever written about Dublin, tells the fictional story of a stunningly beautiful Dublin fishmonger, and it's been popular in Dublin pubs for at least 300 years. In 1988, the city unveiled a statue of the imagined Molly which now stands directly outside the main Tourist Information Center on Grafton Street. If you're into **classic snapshots** (i.e. you have a picture of yourself "leaning" on the Eiffel Tower, and another on the Washington monument), you won't want to miss the opportunity to pose provocatively with Molly Malone.

The Gaelic Games

Ireland has two national sports, and both are played regularly at Croke Park in the northern reaches of central Dublin. If you have the space in your schedule, it's well worth getting in on the action – you'll learn a lot about how Dubliners like to spend their free time. **Gaelic football** is a cousin of American football, and its basic rules will be familiar to anyone who follows rugby or the NFL. **Hurling**, on the other hand, is much less familiar to Americans. Not to be confused with *curling*, the Canadian ice-sweeping competition, this brutal and fast-paced warrior game hovers somewhere between hockey, baseball, and lacrosse, with a healthy dose of MMA thrown in for good measure. Visit the Gaelic Athletic Association (gaa.ie) for a full explanation of the rules.

By 1916, the British Empire had been in control of Ireland for several centuries, and their increasingly brutal tactics of repression had caused a buildup of resentment among the Irish. For many decades, the island had seen the rise of an Irish Nationalist ("Republican") movement whose members believed that the only way to achieve freedom and justice would be to separate completely from British administration. There had been minor clashes and violent incidents during the preceding decades, but in 1916 the Irish revolutionaries saw what they thought would be their best opportunity to overthrow British rule.

Dublin After the Rising
(public domain image)

With the British distracted by an increasingly desperate fight against the Germans (WWI), the Irish believed that they could make enough of a nuisance of themselves that the British government would grant them independence. On the morning of Easter Monday, 1500 armed revolutionaries stormed the streets of Dublin, taking several strategic buildings. Their leaders gathered in the General Post Office, which was extremely valuable because it was the main hub of communication throughout the city.

Unfortunately, the element of surprise could only last so long, and soon the full force of the British administration was filling the streets. Their artillery battered the General Post Office and other buildings occupied by pro-independence forces, causing the sort of mass destruction seen in the photograph. Hopelessly outgunned, the Nationalists were forced to surrender and their leaders were summarily executed.

The failure of the Easter Rising resulted in increased repression by the British. But despite nearly constant hangings and frequent torture of captured revolutionaries, the Nationalists continued pushing for independence.

They would finally rise up en masse in 1919, launching a bloody war that resulted in an equally bloody crackdown. They would ultimately win independence for Ireland – minus the six counties that now make up Northern Ireland.

These seminal events in Irish history are depicted in two excellent (though bleak) films that are highly recommended for anyone interested in Irish history:

Michael Collins (1996) starring Liam Neeson

The Wind That Shakes the Barley (2006) starring Cillian Murphy

Dublin doesn't always feel like a major European capital, but when it comes to food there's no mistaking the high-end international flavor of this place. If you want sushi, Thai, Mediterranean, Central American, Indian, or modern American food, you should have no trouble finding it. To save space, though, this section will focus on restaurants that serve more traditional Irish food. You've come all the way to Ireland, why not taste something local?

Food in Dublin tends to be a little expensive, with the cheapest restaurants charging somewhere in the range of €8-10 for a main course. (However, you can often save money by finding a "BYOB" restaurant, since wine is often the priciest part of your meal.) Of course, the expense comes with both value and variety: you'll find pretty much any kind of cuisine you want here, and usually with very high quality. You can also find high-end dining here, including the Michelin-rated **Restaurant Patrick Guilbaud**, which at two stars out of three is perhaps the most critically acclaimed restaurant in the country.

Traditional Irish Meals

Arguably the best place to get a traditional meal is in one of the pubs listed in the next section, since these places tend to have excellent kitchens and fairly reasonable prices. However, if the pub atmosphere is not for you, here are a few restaurants where you can get authentic Irish fare in a little more of a "restaurant" setting:

Gallagher's Boxty House (20 Temple Bar)

A small, intimate Irish restaurant serving stew, chowder, and of course boxties (fried po-tato pancakes rolled up around a meat or vegetable filling and served with rich gravy).

Johnnie Fox's (Glencullen Road)

Well outside the city, but well worth the trip. Situated on a hill outside Dublin, this restaurant specializes in fresh seafood and offers great city views. With its regular musical acts and boisterous conversation, it's closer to the pub atmosphere than most.

Cornucopia (19 Wicklow Street)

There's really no such thing as a "vegetarian option" in the traditional Irish diet. Historically, if you weren't eating meat it was because you couldn't afford to. Nowadays, pretty much every Irish meal includes a healthy dose of animal protein. So the options at Cornucopia aren't exactly the most *authentic* in the city. They are, however, quite delicious and not too expensive, and the restaurant is a godsend for vegans and vegetarians on this highly carnivorous island.

Ryan's FXB (Parkgate Street)

Good mid-range option serving seafood and steaks near the Guinness Storehouse. For about €20-30, you can taste some of Ireland's choicest cuts of meat.

Pubs & Clubs

Dublin is rightly famous for its drinking scene. At one end of the spectrum, you'll find traditional pubs with a relaxed, earthy atmosphere — many of them claiming to be over 1,000 years old! At the other end of the spectrum are Dublin's many nightclubs, which generally cater to a young, international clientele. Young people from all over Europe flock to Dublin's clubs to dance, giving them a global, pan-European feel. And all along that spectrum, you'll find plenty of Guinness, fine whiskey, and *craic* (Irish for camaraderie and boisterous conversation).

Traditional Pubs

There are many claims to the title of **Dublin's oldest pub**, and no one knows for sure which one is true. The most common answer is **the Brazen Head**, established in 1198. With its intimate setting, the Brazen Head is also one of Dublin's best venues for traditional music. Ordinarily there will be a "trad" band playing lively tunes in a corner, but even when there are no musicians onstage, the patrons will frequently break out into traditional Irish folk songs, which can be a truly sublime musical experience. Between the timeless music, the beer, and the worn stone walls, it's easy to feel like you've stepped into a place that is immune to the passage of time.

Whether or not the Brazen Head is in fact the oldest pub in Dublin, it has certainly preserved its historic feel better than most. Here, though, are a few of the other contenders:

The Celt (81 Talbot Street)

Renowned for its nightly music sessions and an excellent kitchen.

An Conradh (6 Harcourt Street)

An Irish-language pub, popular with Irish-speaking locals (tragically, a dwindling population). Whereas many of the traditional pubs in Ireland are heavily patronized by tourists, this one tends to be more popular with locals.

Mulligan's (Poolbeg Street)

One of James Joyce's favorite spots in Dublin, and a great place to learn about Irish whiskeys, as the bartenders there are especially knowledgeable.

Kehoe's (South Anne Street)

Just off Grafton Street, so convenient for tourists. It's great if you want to try having dinner in a "snug," the tiny rooms offered for the privacy and comfort of patrons. (Historically, snugs were frequently used by revolutionaries planning various uprisings against the British.)

Clubs

For one of the largest parties in the country, head to **The Button Factory** (Curved Street, Temple Bar). With a capacity of over 700 and a rotating roster of international DJs, it's a great place to mingle with students and backpackers from around the world.

Krystle (Harcourt Street)

This is one of Dublin's more elite nightclubs. Expensive drinks, wealthy local celebrities, and a decidedly exclusive atmosphere.

Twisted Pepper (54 Middle Abbey Street)

On the weekends, this is a student club more or less like any other, but during the week it caters to hardcore lovers of electronic dance music.

The Dragon (64 South Georges Street)

A relaxed, gay-friendly club with some of the best cocktails in the city.

Temple Bar District

Located just south of the river in the very heart of Dublin, the Temple Bar is famous (some might say infamous) as the **party capital** of Ireland. Its bars are some of the most popular in the country, and the streets practically flow with beer and whiskey. On weekends, the party often spills out into the streets around midnight. It's a long way from the traditional drinking environment of a place like the Brazen Head, but it's a great way to mingle with locals and fellow travelers alike.

Early Evening around Temple Bar
(photo credit: Trevah via Wikimedia Commons)

For many years, there was no actual bar called "Temple Bar." It was a good way to catch people out, actually – if they asked you how to get to "the actual bar," or asked a question like "how's the drinking at the Temple Bar," you'd know they didn't know the area very well. Now, however, there actually is a place called **The Temple Bar**, at the corner of Essex Street and Temple Lane.

One of the best and most dangerous things about pubs in the Temple Bar district is that many of them have **in-table beer taps**. That means you don't have to go up to the bar to order another round. Just grab the handle and pull! Beware: when the tap is in the middle of your table, you will find yourself drinking A LOT more than you normally would, which is occasionally unsafe, and almost always extremely expensive. The bar keeps track of how much beer your table pours for itself, and they will charge you a premium at the end of the night. Treat the tap as you would a hotel mini-bar – go nuts if you can afford it, but otherwise steer clear.

If you're walking around in the Temple Bar, you can't throw a stick without hitting a hen or stag party (what we call bachelor and bachelorette parties). These large, single-gender groups move from pub to pub and party continuously in a raucous manner that puts the average bachelor/ette party to shame. If you see a large group in any bar in this district, chances are one of them is getting married in the morning – be careful who you flirt with!

Festival Participant in Dublin
(photo credit: Miguel Mendez via Creative Commons)

Festivals in Dublin

If you're planning a trip to Dublin, don't miss out on the opportunity to see some of the city's famous festivals. The universal Irish love of celebration extends well beyond St. Patrick's Day and encompasses a huge number of other party days and festivals. Just like any other major city, Dublin sets aside days and even whole weeks to celebrate food, music, drink, dance, culture, and various historical events.

Dublin Restaurant Week, for example, takes place at the end of March and gives restaurateurs throughout the city an opportunity to give out samples and serve all sorts of delicacies to visitors and neighbors alike. This is not just a fun festival event, either – for the savvy tourist, it's also an opportunity to sample the culinary possibilities of Dublin and maybe decide which restaurants to eat at during the trip!

Dublin also hosts countless music festivals, especially for Irish traditional and folk music. In late May, for example, music lovers from all over Ireland congregate in the little town of Skerries, about a half-hour's drive north of the city. The weekend-long festival focuses specifically on the unique musical culture of the eastern counties. Whereas most traditional music festivals in Dublin combine music from all over the island, the **Skerries Music Festival** is a rare opportunity to delve more deeply into a specific regional style.

But of course no festival is more important than **St. Patrick's Day**. This day of celebration has become a global phenomenon, and the Irish love to welcome travelers and tourists – both those of Irish heritage and those who simply appreciate the island's culture. The city holds a massive parade of musicians, artists, street performances, public officials, huge troupes of dancers, and local businesses. It's an overwhelming experience! You'll also find great deals and special events at businesses throughout the city, especially the Guinness Storehouse, which holds a 3-day special event in the center of the city. If you enjoy festivities (and you're not afraid of big crowds) there's no better time to visit Dublin than St. Patrick's Day.

The majority of festivals in Dublin (and throughout the country) happen between late March and early July, making these months the most popular with tourists. For some people, this is part of the appeal – for others, it's a disaster. Time your trip according to your own tastes!

CULTURE NOTE:
St. Patrick's, Shamrocks, and the "Luck of the Irish"

On St. Patrick's Day, as the saying goes, everyone is Irish for a day. But how do people in Ireland actually celebrate their national holiday? In many ways the local celebrations, especially in major cities, are similar to those around the world – parades, music, beer, and large numbers of people dressed in green. Naturally, the Irish themselves are even more excited about the day than those in other countries, and schools and businesses (except bars and restaurants!) are generally closed for the festivities.

St. Patrick's Day festivities in Ireland vary tremendously from town to town. Dublin puts on the biggest show in the country, of course, and the grandeur of the festivities attract huge numbers of travelers. These travelers, though, affect the celebration pretty dramatically as the city attempts to give them the sort of experience that they're expecting – some people consider this gaudy and inauthentic, and prefer to spend St. Patrick's Day in smaller towns. For sheer spectacle, though, Dublin is hard to beat!

In smaller towns, especially those in the western counties, the celebration may be on a smaller scale, but it's still fervent and full of life. Many of these towns actually have **two separate parades**. One, held around dawn, sees smaller crowds (and almost no tourists) turning out for traditional music and conversation before Mass. A second parade in the late afternoon is more raucous and closer to what Americans and other outsiders are accustomed to. In the evenings, men and women crowd the local bars to sing, drink, and celebrate their shared heritage.

But in addition to its status as a cultural festival and a day of revelry, St. Patrick's Day is also one of the most important religious holidays in Ireland. St. Patrick himself, who lived in the 5th century AD, was a child slave who became a missionary and, according to legend, helped convert the Celts to Christianity by using a **shamrock** to explain the concept of the Holy Trinity. This is why the shamrock, with three leaves, is among the national emblems of Ireland – the four-leaf clover, on the other hand, is a different plant that has nothing to do with Ireland, contrary to the belief of some people in America. (Lucky Charms cereal confused the two plants in 1964, and Americans have been repeating their mistake ever since.)

Incidentally, this confusion over clovers led to a further confusion over the common expression "**luck of the Irish**." In the 1800s, when half-starved famine victims were flooding into America, they were seen as hapless and pitiable – someone who had the "luck of the Irish" had no luck at all. No one knows exactly when Americans inverted the meaning of the phrase, but it was right around the 1960s, and it's quite possible that Lucky Charms cereal was, once again, to blame for the mistake.

The story of St. Patrick chasing the snakes out of Ireland is a popular allegory for his converting the pagans and polytheists. For pious Catholics in Ireland, St. Patrick's Day is a moment for prayer, reflection, and gratitude to the saint who brought them their religion – but they'll still happily participate in all the secular aspects of the celebration as well.

Outside Dublin

Dublin definitely dominates the tourism scene in Leinster, but there are many excellent sites outside the city that are well worth a visit while you're in the area.

Neolithic Ireland

Newgrange Main Entrance
(photo credit: Clemensfranz via Wikimedia Commons)

What were the Irish Celts up to in the fourth millennium BC, when the Egyptians were busy with their pyramids? It turns out they were building some pretty impressive monuments of their own, though most are no longer standing. Eastern Ireland is full of archaeological sites where these monuments are being unearthed, studied, and, in some cases, reconstructed.

Perhaps the best example is **Newgrange**, a UNESCO World Heritage Site in County Meath, about 40 minutes' drive from Dublin. This site has been meticulously rebuilt into a perfect replica of how archaeologists believe it looked 5,000 years ago, when it was new. The reconstruction uses original stones from the site, so visitors can see the intricate, spiraling designs of the Celtic religion carved into stones whose spiritual significance we can only guess at.

Like many Neolithic Celtic sites, Newgrange is a prime example of primitive astronomy: the monument was constructed in such a way that the rising sun would illuminate its inner chamber on the Winter Solstice, and on no other day of the year.

Wicklow Mountains National Park

Wicklow Mountains
(photo credit: J.H. Janssen via Wikimedia Commons)

Leinster is hardly renowned for its hiking – unlike the west of Ireland, it was not carved by powerful ocean winds, but rather consists of a gently rolling landscape more reminiscent of the English countryside. However, there is a large national park about 7 miles south of Dublin that breaks this rule. The peaks of Wicklow Mountains National Park are not as dramatic as those of Kerry or Donegal, but they have the advantage of easy accessibility from Dublin, and they are rarely frequented by tourists.

In addition, the Wicklow Mountains extend for an area of over 1,000 square miles, making them one of Ireland's largest uninterrupted stretches of wilderness. Gentle to moderate hiking will get you to stunning vistas, cool mountain lakes, and plenty of quiet solitude.

Believed to be **Ireland's oldest living settlement**, the city of Waterford (population 46,000) was founded by Vikings at roughly the same time as Dublin (ca. 900 AD). It's distinctly proud of this long history, and there are plenty of historic sites and museums to visit. Waterford is right on the boundary between Leinster and Munster, so it's a great stop on roadtrips from eastern Ireland to the vast countryside of the South.

Given its relatively large size (yes, 46,000 counts as a pretty big town in Ireland), and its location halfway between the tourist-heavy cities of Dublin and Cork, you might expect that Waterford would have become a major tourist destination in its own right. But this has not happened. It's actually retained a lot of its traditional **small-town charm**. This is one of the advantages of visiting this town – you'll get an authentic feel for the seemingly timeless small Irish town.

Part III
Connacht

In a quiet corner of County Roscommon, one of the most rural and rarely-traveled parts of Connacht, there's a little gully leading into a small stone cave. It catches water and occasionally the local sheep will drink from it, but other than that it's rarely noticed. There are no signs or plastic fences to control visiting crowds (which, anyway, aren't congregating here in the first place). To the uninitiated, it looks like a perfectly nondescript little hole in the ground.

But once a year, the spirits of this cave swarm up out of the ground and walk the earth for a single night in late autumn. For this cave, according to ancient Irish mythology, is the entrance to **the underworld**. And on the festival of *Samhain* (SAH-wain), its doors stand open for a night. This pagan festival would eventually evolve into the holiday of Halloween. But the cave at the center of it all was largely forgotten, and today you can walk right into it, right up to the threshold of the Celtic spirit world. (The cave is called Oweynagat, and it's located at Rathcroghan just outside the town of Tulsk, if you're interested.)

Oweynagat isn't the only mythical site in Connacht, or even in County Roscommon alone. Seemingly every plot of land in this corner of the island is dotted with the ruined fortresses of mythical kings and queens, or with stone rings thought to be inhabited by the *sidhe*, the original fairy-folk of Irish lore.

But don't get the wrong impression – Connacht is not an antiquarian backwater. It's an extremely vibrant center of Irish cultural life, and home to one of Ireland's greatest cities. If Dublin is the economic and social center of Ireland, **Galway** is its beating Gaelic heart. Music, art, dance, food, and education are the specialties in this compact, energetic city.

That's why so many travelers fall in love with Connacht. In the heart of Galway, you can surround yourself with raucous company and take in all the sites of a modern city – but just a few miles down the road you can get lost in the timeless mysteries of nature, history, and myth.

Getting Into Connacht

If you're coming to Connacht for a visit, you're almost certainly getting there by way of Galway. As Ireland's "second city," Galway is easily accessible by **train** or **bus** from Dublin (the train, of course, is considerably faster and more comfortable, but slightly more expensive).

Some travelers target Connacht and the western counties for their trip, meaning they prefer to skip Dublin altogether. In this case, you have two options. **Knock Airport** in County Mayo is relatively small, but is rapidly growing - as of 2015, there are direct flights to Knock from New York City and many cities in Europe. The more tried-and-true option is **Shannon Airport** in nearby County Clare (just south of Connacht). Both airports are about a 2-hour bus and/or train ride away from the city of Galway.

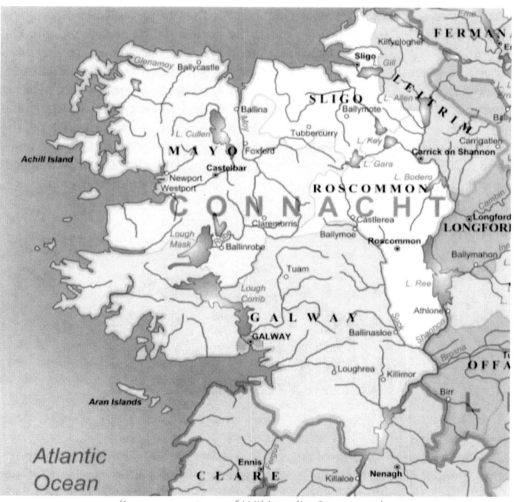

(image courtesy of Wikimedia Commons)

Located in County Galway in southern Connacht, Galway is rightly praised as the cultural capital of Ireland, and is the main travel hub for anyone passing through Connacht. With its stunning combination of artistic, musical, and athletic events (to say nothing of the rousing nightlife), Galway has become one of Ireland's most popular destinations, not only with international tourists but also with vacationers from elsewhere in Ireland. Galway also has the advantage of being right in the middle of some of the most stunning green landscapes on the Emerald Isle, and makes a perfect home base for hikers, backpackers, and campers.

After music and dance, Galway is known primarily for one thing: its **pubs**. Although the pubs in Galway are less historic than those in Dublin (the oldest are *only* four or five centuries old!), they are bursting with *craic* and the traditional Irish pub atmosphere. The pubs often play host to Galway's storied session musicians. Like New Orleans or Chicago in the United States, Galway has been the ultimate destination for several generations of aspiring musicians, and an incredible scene has formed around these musicians and their fans. Although the Galway music scene is definitely centered on the traditional music of western Ireland, it also has plenty of jazz, rock, and blues bands. This diversity of musical sounds, mingling with the sounds of laughter and revelry, is the constant backbeat of life in Ireland's cultural capital.

Calm Afternoon on Galway Bay
(photo credit: J. Diego via Creative Commons)

Galway's location on the **coast** is also a draw for tourists. But remember — this is Ireland's western coast. Galway Bay offers a little shelter, but not much, and the pounding fury of the Atlantic is definitely a feature of life here. The Galway coast has its share of sandy beaches, but the weather is infamously unpredictable and overpowering winds can put a quick end to any planned day of sunbathing. In addition, capricious rain-storms can roll in without any warning whatsoever, and sometimes you'll even experience a torrential downpour coming out of a clear blue sky. It's surreal and eerily beautiful in its own way, but still it's best to plan on getting wet if you plan to spend much time outside, especially in Spring and Fall. However, all this confusion and intermittent rain has a great upside – in the right seasons, you're likely to see a rainbow almost every day hanging over the Galway skyline.

Getting Around in Galway

Galway is very compact and easily walkable. And, of course, the advantage of walking is amplified by the beautiful views and fresh sea air. Most visitors won't need to set foot inside a motor vehicle from the time they arrive in Galway to the time they leave. But if you do need to make a longer trip (or if you're simply tired from a long day of walking) you have two options. Local **bus** networks cover the city fairly comprehensively, although you will probably wait longer for a bus than you would in Dublin. You can also **hail a cab** fairly easily in central areas such as Bridge Street and around the Cathedral.

Key Sights in Galway

Spanish Arch

Though it doesn't look like much today, Galway's Spanish Arch is one of the last remaining remnants of the city's defensive wall, constructed back in the 16th Century. Today, it's a pleasant part of the seaside roadway known as the Long Walk. Its proximity to the Galway City Museum makes it a convenient stop for travelers strolling coastal Galway.

Galway City Museum

This **free** museum appeals to history buffs, children, and anyone interested in Irish art and culture. It has a wide range of artifacts and displays covering every aspect of Galway's heritage. Also a nice, compact venue for musical performances, which are scheduled fairly regularly and are always well worth an evening's listen.

The Cathedral from Bridge St.
(photo credit: Phalinn via Creative Commons)

Galway Cathedral

The cathedral is a beautiful building situated just off Bridge Street in the northern area of central Galway. For-mally known as **The Cathedral of Our Lady Assumed into Heaven and St Nicholas**, it's among the youngest of Europe's major cathedrals, having been constructed in 1958. Whereas most of the cathedrals and churches in Ireland display a fairly traditional Gothic style of architecture, this one has a much more eclectic style, combining Spanish and Romanesque influences.

Salthill

Situated about a mile to the southwest of central Galway is the little neighborhood of Salthill. Once a quiet seaside suburb, Salthill has seen significant development over the last couple of decades, and is hardly recognizable from its former self. The advantage of this development is that there are now plenty of things for tourists to do in Salthill, notably a very pleasant **seaside promenade** and one of Connacht's few sandy beaches. Between the frigid waters and unpredictable weather, this is hardly a sunbather's paradise. You're not in Brazil, after all. But the beach is remarkably free of crowds, and on those sunny days in late summer when the water briefly warms up, you can have all the sand and surf to yourself!

The Saturday Market

Every Saturday for seemingly as long as anyone can remember, Saturdays have been Market Day in Galway. From 8am to around 6pm each week, **Church Lane** transforms into a bustling marketplace. Dozens of merchants sell seasonal goods, souvenirs, and foods of every kind. Since Galway is such a crossroads of modern globalization and traditional Irish culture, it should come as no surprise that the selection at the Saturday Market is extremely eclectic – at one stall you'll find a man selling locally-produced cheeses, while his neighbor may be selling Spanish olives or crêpes as soft and flavorful as any you'd find in Paris. (Insider tip: don't miss the **sausage cart**, especially during winter – their small, spicy sausages are outstanding, and there's no better way to stave off the cold.) There's also a smaller and shorter Market Day on Sunday afternoons, but the selection tends to be more limited.

Traditional Music

If you're going to be spending any time in Ireland's cultural capital, it would be a shame to leave without taking in any of the city's incredible musical delights. This might include an evening at **The Crane**, a tiny West End pub that has gained a reputation as the city's best venue for traditional music. **Monroe's Tavern** also has a roaring "trad fest" every single night of the week. If you want to learn a little Irish set dancing, stop by on Tuesday nights to watch and learn. There's also **Taafles**, centrally located near the main shopping district and open most hours of the day and night. A great way to take in some music if you aren't so much of a night owl.

Irish Arts

Of course, nothing goes with music quite so well as art – and Galway has plenty of both. The City Museum is one of the best places to see traditional art, while the **Galway Arts Centre** (just off Bridge Street) houses a large gallery showcasing more contemporary art from Ireland and beyond. The Centre also puts on excellent classes and workshops.

Where to Stay

Being a major hub of both domestic and international tourism, Galway is packed with hotels to match any budget. Youth hostels such as **Kinlay House** and the **Galway City Hostel** (both centrally located near Eyre Square and the Galway Train Station) have expert staff, mostly local, who can direct you to the best places to eat, drink, and take in the city's sights.

At the other end of the spectrum are luxury hotels, although the best high-end experience will probably come from one of the city's hundreds of **B&B's**. These tiny institutions offer home-cooked meals and a much more personal touch than the standard high-rise hotel, which hasn't really caught on in Galway. You can find very pricey B&B's around Galway that will truly pamper everyone in your group, or slightly more down-to-earth options that pretty much feel like spending the night in the guestroom of some extraordinarily hospitable cousin.

As far as geography goes, the advice is fairly predictable: if you choose a place in the central areas of Galway like **Eyre Square** or the area around **Nun's Island**, you'll be right in the heart of the action – but a quiet escape may be a little harder to find. On the other hand, if you stay in the more suburban areas like **Ballyloughane Strand** or **Shantalia**, you'll have quieter evenings but a slightly less convenient trip into the city. **Salthill** has plenty of hotels, and its atmosphere is somewhere in between the two extremes. Bear in mind, though, that Galway is already a fairly small town by American standards. Pretty much anywhere you stay will be relatively quiet and relatively close.

Where to Eat

Galway's culinary options are decidedly less global than those in cosmopolitan Dublin. The upside, though, is that it's much easier to find real, authentic Irish cuisine. Of course, the **Saturday Market** (see previous page) is a great option on weekends, and definitely more lively than an ordinary restaurant! But Galway also has plenty of restaurants serving a variety of Irish favorites:

Oscar's Restaurant (Upper Dominick St.)
Unassuming little place, but it packs in a lot of flavor. Particularly well known for its local seafood, Oscar's offers a piled-high seafood platter that's great for sharing.

Lohans (Upper Salthill)

One of the more traditional restaurants in Galway. Serves local favorites such as Guinness stew, bacon & cabbage, and of course plenty of sausage and mashed potatoes.

McDonagh's Seafood (22 Quay St.)

You want great fish & chips, and you don't want to pay too much for it. You go to McDonagh's.

The Galleon (Monksfield Rd., Salthill)

The best burger in Ireland. Tender and juicy, made with high-quality Irish beef and served to order with a selection of toppings. OK, the hamburger is maybe not the most *traditional* of Irish foods, but it's quite popular on the island, and no one does it better than the Galleon. This small restaurant also serves a pretty diverse menu of Irish, American, and international dishes. For the most Irish experience, put the chef in charge by ordering a mixed grill or seafood platter.

Pubs & Clubs

Galway doesn't have much to offer in terms of its club scene (that's Dublin's specialty), but it does have some of the best pubs in the world, as well as some great music venues.

Busker Browne's

This is one of the largest bars in Galway and, at about 400, one of the oldest still standing. Live music most nights of the week, a vast selection of beers, and plenty of *craic*. Generally more frequented by backpackers and vacationers than locals, it's a great place to meet new friends and traveling companions.

Cooke's Thatch Bar

Most of Galway's traditional thatched-roof bars have been crowded out by more modern construction, but Cooke's is still standing, and its unrivaled trad sessions are some of the best music in all of Ireland. Walking in, you'll feel as if this place hasn't changed for 200 years, except for the photographs on the wall and the absence of a thick blanket of smoke (indoor smoking was banned in Ireland back in 2004, forever altering the atmosphere of its pubs).

Bierhaus

As its name suggests, Bierhaus is Galway's attempt to emulate a German drinking hall. It serves a huge selection of craft beers as well as local Irish favorites, and features a rotating roster of DJs and electronic music.

Monroe's Tavern

Traditional music most nights of the week, and on Tuesdays a rollicking evening of set dancing. Dancers here tend to be fairly experienced, but if you're patient you may find someone willing to show you the steps.

Roisin Dubh

Named for one of the most popular Irish folk songs, this modern venue hosts rock bands, stand-up comedians, and alternative bands from all over the world — it's a nice juxtaposition with the trad sessions that generally dominate Galway's music scene. (It's pronounced "RO-shin DOVE")

Getting Out of Galway: the Connemara Countryside

Head north from Galway, and you'll immediately find yourself in the sparsely-populated and mostly wild hinterland known as Connemara. It's a sprawling open space of glacial lakes, massive boulders, and sharp-sided mountains unlike any other place on earth. And from late spring to early fall, it shimmers with some of the most vibrant green foliage you'll ever lay eyes on.

If you plan to spend any time in Connemara, bear in mind that it's one of the prouder areas within the Gaeltacht (the Gaelic-speaking part of Ireland – see p. 37), and locals, especially of the older generations, will greatly appreciate any effort you make to speak with them in the Irish language. Of course, they're universally fluent in English, so you'll be able to get by without much trouble. But it's a great way to feel connected to the proud Irish community that calls this beautiful countryside home.

Getting In & Getting Around

There's no rail connection to Connemara, so you'll have to take the train to Galway and then take either a bus, cab, or sightseeing tour to get in. By **bus**, the journey is about 2 hours, but buses leave multiple times each day and there are a couple of different routes available depending on your specific destination. Many local drivers lead **day trips** from Galway that will pick you up in the morning, drive you to some of the best sights in Connemara, then drop you off again before dinner. (A few even make the drive all the way from Dublin!) This is a quick and efficient way to take in the countryside, but of course it won't give you the full experience that an extended stay can offer.

Once you're in Connemara, there are a few bus lines running between the major cities and the National Park, but it's often easier just to **hire a cab**. Cab drivers are extremely knowledgeable about the area, and adept at navigating the narrow mountainside roads of this region. Renting a car is not recommended, since these roads can often give foreign drivers a bit of a panic attack – especially if they're accustomed to lanes, signage, and guardrails, none of which are easily found in rural Connemara.

Connemara National Park

The heart of Connemara – and its most popular destination for hiking, biking, and walking – is the National Park about 40 miles from Galway near the border of County Mayo. It offers some of Ireland's most scenic hiking, and the mountains are generally a bit gentler than those of Kerry or Donegal. You can get spectacular views without a backbreaking journey along the way.

The National Park itself is short on accommodations, but there are several hotels in the nearby town of **Letterfrack**, which is right on the edge of the park. There's also a youth hostel right in the middle of the mountains that makes an ideal base for hikers and backpackers.

Clew Bay from the South
(photo credit: Paul McIlroy via Creative Commons)

Sometimes known as the Twelve Pins, this arc of small mountains skirts the southern edge of Connemara National Park, and its many trails are ideal for day hikes. The mountains offer breathtaking views of Lough Inaugh. There's also a **restaurant** nearby called the Twelve Bens, which offers some of the region's best seafood (though it's a hair outside the price range of the average backpacker).

Clew Bay

Just north of Connemara, in the southern reaches of County Mayo, you'll find Clew Bay, a small inlet with hundreds of **sunken drumlins**, tiny islands undulating up from underwater roots. These islands are the cousins of the low hills surrounding the bay, and create spec-tacular views. Clew Bay is especially popular for sea kayaking – since most of the islands are uninhabited, and entirely undeveloped, they make a perfect destination for exploring and picnicking.

The Aran Islands

A small chain of islands, steeped in legend and surpassing natural beauty, stretches across the mouth of Galway Bay. Known as the Aran Islands, they are some of Ireland's best destinations for nature, history, wildlife, and culture, and their remoteness makes them relatively undiscovered and less frequented by foreign tourists. (Given that the islands themselves have a permanent population of only 900, however, the tourists usually outnumber the locals during the high season!)

Ferries to the Aran Islands leave from Charraroe (County Galway) and Lisdoonvarna (County Clare) several times a day, and are the only way to get in or out. Within the Aran Islands, there are internal ferries between the three major islands, and charter boats can take you to the smaller islands at the northern end of the chain. The largest of the islands is only 8 miles from end to end, so they're all easily walkable.

Like Connemara, the Aran Islands are part of the *Gaeltacht*, so you'll probably hear more Irish than English among the locals. Road signs will also be primarily in Irish, so it's helpful to know place names and words like "stop" (*stad*) before you go.

Kilronan and Killeany

There are two small towns on the northern shore of **Inis Mór** (pronounced "*Innish More*"), the largest of the Aran Islands. They sit on opposite sides of a small bay, and they're the main hub for ferries in and out of the Aran Islands, so these twin villages will probably be your base of operations for exploring the islands. There are a large number of hotels and B&B's in town, as well as shops and groceries. Guided walking and biking tours generally leave from the villages.

In Kilronan you'll also find the **Aran Sweater Market**, where you can buy the famous hand-made sweaters with unique knitted patterns.

Prehistoric Forts and Dwellings

The Defenses at Dun Aengus
(photo credit: Tuoermin via Wikimedia Commons)

There are several prehistoric structures on the Aran Islands, but by far the most famous is **Dun Aengus** near the northern tip of Inis Mór. The fort was constructed around 1000 BC, and is in remarkably good shape (other than a few sections that have crumbled into the sea). The fort, situated on some of western Ireland's famous coastal cliffs, affords spectacular views of the bay and was obviously a formidable obstacle to attackers. Between its high, thick walls and its wide field of broken-up stones, any visitor can see how difficult it would have been to conquer it with spears and arrows.

There's also a **beehive hut** on the west side of the island, a well-preserved example of how the prehistoric Irish people lived during peacetime.

Inis Meáin and Inis Oírr

Although Inis Mór is by far the largest and most popular of the Aran Islands, you can get well off the beaten path by heading to one of the other two main islands in the chain. Both islands are sparsely populated, but have a handful of hotels and B&B's to stay in. They also have some fairly dramatic coastline (just like Inis Mór), good hiking, and very, very few tourists.

The Burren and the Cliffs of Moher

The Cliffs of Moher

Technically, these world-famous natural landmarks are part of County Clare, and there-fore should be in the section on Munster rather than Connacht. But the best way to explore the Burren and the Cliffs of Moher is from a base of operations in Galway, so we've included them here for the sake of convenience. Like Connemara, these regions are reachable by **day tours** that leave every morning from Galway, but you can also find local accommodations and stay for a few days if you really want to settle in and absorb as much of this incredible landscape as possible.

These stunning shale formations tower dramatically over the pounding waves of Galway Bay, rising to a height of over 700 feet at their highest point. On a clear day, the views from atop these cliffs extended for miles, as far as the Aran Islands and even the distant hills of Connemara. But they arguably look their best when **heavy fog** rolls in from the Atlantic Ocean and the cliffs seem to recede into an eternity of swirling grey. On days like that, it can seem like the lines between land, sea, and sky have begun to dissolve.

In addition to their incredible shape, the cliffs provide shelter for thousands of **seabirds**, including a huge colony of colorful Atlantic Puffins. The best way to see these birds is to get into the water itself – many private companies offer special bird cruises. These trips are not only great for bird-watchers, though. They also afford stunning views of the cliffs from the bottom, which are arguably even more dramatic than the views from above!

Note that the Cliffs of Moher are a natural area and many of the precipices are not roped or fenced off. Only a handful of people have ever fallen off out of thousands of annual tourists – but you don't want to become one of them! Stay on the designated trails and watch your step, especially on windy or rainy days.

The best views are found at the picturesque **O'Brien's Tower**, which was built in 1835 as an observation deck. Even in those days, the Cliffs of Moher were an extremely popular destination for tourists, and Sir Cornelius O'Brien decided to give them an even more spectacular view by building a tower on one of the tallest cliffs. It's only €2 for an adult ticket, and well worth the climb when visibility is good. And even if you don't feel like going up to the top, the tower itself makes for great photography.

Poulnabrone Dolmen
(photo credit: Raúl Corral via Wikimedia Commons)

The Burren

Due west of the Cliffs of Moher, at a distance of about 12 miles, you'll find yourself in The Burren, a desolate and almost entirely uninhabited expanse of exposed rock and short grasses. In some places, The Burren looks more like another planet than a terrestrial wilderness – and this is especially true in winter, when the windswept rock formations are almost devoid of visible plant life. In late spring and early summer, however, the whole area explodes with thousands of wildflowers and, for a few glorious weeks, seems like an impressionist painting come to life.

The Burren is also the location of the **Poulnabrone Dolmen**, an ancient tomb that probably housed the remains of some prehistoric royal family in around the 5th millennium BC. Archaeologists have found the remains of at least 16 adults and 6 children in the burial grounds, including a newborn baby who must have been of extreme social importance. In addition to housing the remains of prehistoric chiefs and their children, it was probably used in Druidic rituals long after its function as a tomb ended.

Lemaneagh Castle

From around 1480 to 1705, the castle was occupied by the O'Brien family (yes, the same ones who built O'Brien's Tower), who are believed to be descendants of Brian Boru, the medieval High King of Ireland. The castle is a dramatic ruin, combining several centuries of architectural styles and representing both the luxurious lifestyle of Irish aristocrats and their deep-seated paranoia.

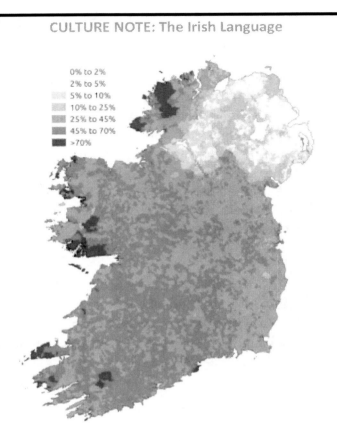

0% to 2%
2% to 5%
5% to 10%
10% to 25%
25% to 45%
45% to 70%
>70%

Visitors are often confused about the national language of Ireland. There are two: **English** is a "secondary official language," whereas the first official language is **Irish**. Many people, especially in America, refer to the Irish language as "**Gaelic**," which is not quite correct since there are many other Gaelic languages such as Scottish Gaelic, Manx, and Breton. However, if you tell an Irishman that you're learning to speak Gaelic, he'll assume that you mean Irish and probably won't be confused. Still, it's best in general to refer to the language as "Irish" (or *gaeilge*, as it's called in the language).

This map shows the percentage of people in Ireland who speak Irish fluently. As you can see, that only accounts for about half of Ireland's population overall, and even those who are fluent generally don't consider Irish their first language. The language has been in a slow decline ever since the British began their conquest of Ireland over 700 years ago, and today it is kept alive through vigorous government action, which makes Irish a mandatory part of the curriculum in all public schools and requires that public employees demonstrate fluency in the language. Pretty much everyone in Ireland is fluent in English, with the possible exception of a few very elderly folks in the western counties.

The dark green regions on the map are known as the *gaeltacht*, or the Irish-speaking portion of Ireland. Heavily concentrated in the western counties of Kerry, Galway, and Donegal, these regions are the last remaining locations where you can hear Irish used as an everyday language in shops and on the street. Though small, these areas are enormously productive in terms of literature and music, which helps to keep the Irish language alive and relevant in the modern world.

Sadly, the younger generation in Ireland generally sees itself as part of a cosmopolitan, unified Europe, and they don't show as much interest in the Irish language as their parents and grandparents did. But as long as public efforts to sustain the language remain strong, it will stay alive and its ancient literary and cultural heritage will not be lost to the world.

Sligo

The Sligo Coastline
(photo credit: Aonghus Flynn via Wikimedia Commons)

The sparsely-populated countryside of County Sligo (northern Connacht) inspired much of William Butler Yeats's poetry, and is still a hugely overlooked destination among travelers today. The gentle undulations of the coastline are far less dramatic than those in the rest of western Ireland, but they have an understated tranquility that brings its own pleasures. And as you move away from the coast, you enter the gently rolling farmlands that stretch out from the wilderness of Connemara up to the moun-tains of Donegal. It's a magical location where you'll find very few tourists – other than the occasional literary pilgrim coming to see the muses of the great poet Yeats himself.

Getting In and Where to Stay

County Sligo is about a 3-hour train ride from Dublin, and is also served by several bus lines – all operating through Sligo Town in the northern part of the county. Flights to the region come through **Knock Airport** in nearby County Mayo. You can also drive in, but (like the rest of rural Ireland) this region has extremely narrow, winding, and poorly-maintained roads. Be prepared to negotiate difficult curves, and don't be surprised if you end up waiting for a stubborn herd of sheep to cross the road.

The majority of hotels, hostels, and B&B's are found in Sligo Town (population 19,000) and along the Sligo coastline. There's also the **Gyreum Ecolodge**, a tiny hilltop hostel in the remote southern reaches of the county – this is one of the few accommodations available to adventurous travelers who want to hike the largely untraveled hills of inland Sligo.

Mountains

Perhaps the most iconic mountain in County Sligo is **Benbulben**, a huge flat-topped table mountain overlooking Sligo Bay. Benbulben recently gained international fame as a prominent part of the backdrop in the critically-acclaimed film *Calvary*. Although it contributes a lot of character to the coastline, however, the slopes are generally too steep for climbing. There is a single path up to the top, which is a relatively strenuous climb, and of course some people attempt the hand-over-hand technical climb straight up the rock face.

The best hiking in Sligo is probably up **Knocknarea**, a half-hour or so climb from bottom to top. Knocknarea is just a couple of miles west of Sligo, on the other side of the bay from Benbulben. In addition to spectacular views the summit also has the famous **Knocknarea Cairn**, a massive pile of stones brought up from the bottom by thousands of travelers over the years. The cairn is believed to be the burial site of one of the most fearsome villains in all of Irish mythology: Queen Medb (pronounced "MAY-v" – welcome to spelling in the Irish language). If you do visit the cairn, **don't** climb on it or damage it in any way, as this is an extremely important cultural heritage site. However, local custom recommends that travelers bring a pebble or small stone from the bottom of the mountain to add to the pile. Mistreatment of the cairn, or failure to bring such an offering, could result in Queen Medb haunting your nightmares until she exacts her revenge.

Yeats Country

Lovers of literature will find a lot to get excited about in Ireland, and when it comes to poetry there are few more exciting destinations than the many sites that inspired W.B. Yeats. Locals are so proud of having inspired this great poet that the entire region around Sligo Town is sometimes referred to as Yeats Country. The sites discussed by the poet include **Dooney Rock Forest**, a small parkland on the shores of Lough Gill, as well as **Innisfree**, a small island in the middle of the lake whose tantalizing distance from the shore inspired one of Yeats's most famous lines: *"I will arise and go now, and go to Innisfree."*

Carrowmore Cemetery
(photo credit: Jon Sullivan via Creative Commons)

Monolithic Cemeteries

There are two monolithic cemeteries near Sligo Town, called **Carrowmore** and **Carrowkeel**. Carrowmore, the more im-portant of the two from an archaeological perspective, is a massive passage tomb complex consisting of a central dolmen with several satellite tombs facing toward the center. One of the tombs has been reconstructed so that visitors can see what it might have looked like when it was new, and the tomb complex as a whole has an excellent Visitor's Center where you can learn all about the prehistoric civilization that built these magnificent tombs.

If County Sligo is known for just one thing, it's traditional music – especially a traditional Connacht variety of Irish music that emphasizes high-speed, intensely virtuosic fiddling. Although some of the more famous Sligo fiddlers end up playing in Sligo Town, you can often hear incredibly talented players in the tiny pubs and inns of rural southern Sligo. Because of the lack of mountains and archaeological sites, people in southern Sligo are not used to seeing tourists, but if you tell them you've come to hear their music, most people will happily direct you to their favorite venue. If you see them later in the pub, you can thank them for their advice by offering to buy them a drink.

Part IV: Munster (The South)

Munster is vast, sparsely populated, and full of small, diverse regional cultures as distinct from one another as Galway is from Dublin. It has relatively few large cities, but it's full of spectacular countryside and wilderness, from the gleaming coastline of Galley Head to the towering mountains of the Iveragh Peninsula.

Due to its large size and the spread-out configuration of its major tourist sites, there's no single way to enter or visit Munster. If your base of operations is in Cork, you'll have one set of options; in Limerick or County Clare, the options will be completely different.

If you're exploring Munster, be sure to check out the information on The Burren and the Cliffs of Moher in the previous section, as these sites are part of Munster and fairly easy to access from Limerick.

(image courtesy of Wikimedia Commons)

As Munster's largest city and the second largest in the Republic of Ireland, Cork is a city of spectacular culture, unbelievable food, and a long and storied history. It's a veritable mecca of backpackers from all over Europe and the United States, and also hosts plenty of more upscale visitors in its high-end hotels and restaurants. The local campus, **University College Cork**, is one of the largest in the region, so Cork definitely has the feel of a college town.

Getting In & Getting Around

Cork Airport is one of the major international airports in Ireland, and has regular flights to and from cities across Britain and Europe. At the moment, there are no direct flights to Cork from anywhere in the United States, so you'll probably end up flying through London or another European city. Alternatively, you could fly into Dublin Airport and take a train, which will add two or three hours to your journey.

If you're already in Ireland, it's very easy to get to Cork by either bus or train, although direct train routes are sometimes tough to find – to get into Cork, you'll probably have to take a train first to Dublin.

Once you're in Cork, the city itself is extremely walkable, and all the key sights are located within about a 1-mile radius of the city center. However, just like Dublin the city has local buses and an excellent **Hop-on Hop-off Bus Tour**. It also has excellent **walking tours** that take in all the major sights with plenty of fresh air and a charming guide along the way.

Where to Stay

Cork is extremely popular with backpackers, so it's full of hostels that run around €10-20 per night. These include the especially inexpensive **Kinlay House** (just north of the river) and the **International Youth Hostel**, a Hostelling International location with a pretty young clientele.

You'll also find mid-range hotels throughout the downtown area, all of which are pretty much interchangeable. A few notable options include the **Silver Springs Morans Hotel**, which has useful business facilities for travelers who need to get work done while on the road. There's also the **Imperial Hotel Cork**, which is the most centrally-located of the mid-range hotels.

For luxury accommodations, you have two options within the city, plus several others some distance away. The more convenient luxury options are the **Clarion Hotel**, which offers river views in addition to the usual amenities; and **Hayfield Manor**, Cork's only 5-star hotel.

Eating in Cork

In terms of its culinary scene, Cork is definitely closer to Dublin than it is to Galway – that is, it's highly eclectic and international, but it's sometimes tough to find a real, traditional Irish meal. If you're looking for authenticity, your best option may be to stop in at the local pub and ask if they have a working kitchen. If they don't, they can pro-bably recommend a place that does.

Other notable options include:

Cork English Market (Grand Parade, South Mall)

This traditional covered market feels a lot like the ones you'd find in Britain or even Italy or Spain, but the food is distinctively Irish. Amongst the huge variety of foods on offer here, you'll find plenty of Irish favorites like sausage, stew, and all manner of potatoes.

Fenn's Quay (5 Fenns Quay)

Upscale renditions of traditional Irish favorites alongside more cosmopolitan European fare. It's an excellent family restaurant for those who can afford it, and it has one of the best wine cellars in Cork.

Captain America's Cookhouse and Bar (4-5 South Main Street)

Tacky? Yes. Surreal? Yes. Pretty much the opposite of a traditional Irish meal? Ab-solutely. But the food is actually really good. It's a tiny shrine to American celebrity memorabilia, comic books, movies, and food. Not exactly what you'd call a slice of home, but a fascinating look at the way Ireland views America.

Nightlife in Cork
(photo credit: Erik Charlton via Creative Commons)

Pubs & Clubs

Cork is full of students, and that means one thing – lots and lots of bars. You won't have any trouble finding a place to wet your whistle in this town, although earthy, traditional pubs are less common than rowdy student bars and pulsing nightclubs.

One of the best ways to experience Cork's nightlife (for those up to the task) is the **Cork City Pub Crawl**, which takes place every Friday night and stumbles its way into 4 or 5 pubs before the evening is out. The specific itinerary varies from week to week, so check out their Facebook page if you want updates. On certain evenings, the pub crawl also includes free glowsticks, which tells you a little about the sort of drinkers it attracts.

An Realt Dearg (Elizabeth Fort)

Cork's oldest pub (est. 1698) may be the oldest continuously-operational pub in the country. Several pubs in Dublin, such as the Brazen Head, are much older, but have had interruptions in their service. Naturally, this title is hotly contested, but "The Gateway" (as it was once known) is a solid contender.

An Bróg (Oliver Plunkett St.)

Irish for "The Shoe," this bar in central Cork is wildly popular with the student crowd. Young backpackers love it for the opportunity it affords to connect with locals their own age, but it's generally avoided by the older generation. An eclectic selection of music plays every night of the week.

An Spailpín Fánach (South Main St.)

Arguably the most traditional of all the pubs in Cork in terms of music and atmosphere. It's an excellent place to catch some Irish music in a cozy setting.

FreakScene (South Main St.)

The name tells you a lot about this place. Two levels, packed with gyrating students, pump out indie, electronic music, disco, and R&B. Known as one of the most gay-friendly clubs in Cork, and also famous for the unusual attire favored by some of its patrons.

Long Island Bar (11 Washington St.)

Best place in Cork for cocktails. A huge variety of mixed drinks, expertly prepared, in a fairly typical lounge setting.

Thomond Bar (2 Marlboro St.)

If you want to share in Cork's love of sports, head to Thomond's. Locals congregate here to watch rugby, soccer, cricket, hurling, Irish football, and a bewildering array of lesser-known sports. This ranges from worldwide international soccer matches, through the college and regional levels, all the way down to local Cork teams playing in various Irish sports leagues.

Key Sights in Cork

The Lough

Cork's main public park is known as The Lough, and it surrounds a quiet little limestone pond just a half-mile or so from the city center. Local wildlife frequently congregates in The Lough, giving visitors an opportunity to enjoy a huge variety of birdlife. And, of course, travelers who want to get in a little exercise can hardly do better than a jog around The Lough's picturesque shoreline.

Elizabeth Fort was built in the 17th century as a defensive installation outside the city proper. Despite being just steps away from the massive St. Finbarr's Cathedral, it is actually quite difficult to see from the street, and many tourists miss it altogether. But once you find your way in, you can climb to the top to get the best city view Cork has to offer. Elizabeth Fort also hosts a weekly Market Festival, where local merchants congregate to sell food, handmade souvenirs, and other local goods.

St. Finbarr's Cathedral
(photo credit: Connor Turner via Creative Commons)

St. Finbarr's Cathedral

This awe-inspiring 19th-century cathedral is one of the most striking architectural works in all of southern Ireland. The church is dedicated to Cork's patron saint, the 6th-century monk who is believed to have founded the town around 550, less than a hundred years after St. Patrick died.

Midsummer Festival

If you missed the Irish festival season (spring to early summer), you can still get your fill of festivity at Cork's annual Midsummer Festival, which lasts several weeks and usually ends around the middle of July. It's a celebration of Irish arts and culture, especially music, theater, and the visual arts.

Fitzgerald Park and Cork Public Museum

This park on the riverbank is small but extremely pleasant, with a pond in the center, a children's playground, and plenty of locals playing cricket, soccer, and Gaelic games. At the edge of Fitzgerald Park is the Cork Public Museum, which features exhibits on local history and culture.

How to Visit the Blarney Stone – If you Must

Of all the many popular tourist destinations in Ireland, perhaps the most famous – and undoubtedly the most overrated – is the Blarney Stone outside Cork. Located on the high walls of **Blarney Castle**, the Blarney Stone is supposed to endow the kisser with the gift of flattery and beguiling talk. A popular legend states that local teenagers periodically break into the grounds of Blarney Castle to urinate on the stone. Castle security guards insist that this has never happened, but the popularity of the story is indicative of how much stock the locals put in the legends about the Blarney Stone – to them, it's nothing more than a hugely successful tourist trap.

Blarney Castle, however, is a beautiful structure and well worth a visit in its own right. The castle is in remarkably good condition given its age, and the surrounding grounds include a beautiful and tranquil garden that most visitors skip entirely.

And, OK, the Blarney Stone is an overly commercialized tourist trap – but you may still get a thrill from leaning over the edge to kiss the mossy stone. Besides, lots of people enjoy the sort of obligatory snap shot that you can only get by visiting the Blarney Stone. Just don't mistake it for a genuine Irish cultural site.

America has about 35 million people of Irish descent. The population of the Republic of Ireland is about one-seventh of that number, at just under 5 million. Why are there so many more Irish-Americans than there are Irish citizens? The reason is a tiny fungus called *phytophthora infestans* – also known as the Potato Blight.

In the mid-1800s, Ireland was thoroughly under the domination of the British Empire, which parceled out the fertile land to various aristocratic families. These wealthy, English-speaking Protestants owned nearly all of the land in Ireland, but the people who worked it were poor, Irish-speaking Catholics. Overlapping ethnic, religious, and class tensions were rampant.

While meat, grain, and dairy products were exported to Great Britain or consumed by the landowners, Irish peasants subsisted almost entirely on potatoes, which could be grown on tiny plots of land from a small number of "seed potatoes." It was already a precarious situation, especially in the poorer counties of Munster and Connacht.

Then, in 1845, a virulent strain of potato blight swept across Ireland and nearly wiped out the potato crop. Within the space of a single year, hunger scoured the landscape like a wildfire, and many people resorted to eating their seed potatoes – meaning they had nothing to plant the following year. In the years 1845-1849, the Catholic population of Ireland was cut nearly in half due to a combination of starvation and mass emigration, primarily to the land of opportunity: America. Anyone who could book passage or stow away on a merchant ship bound for America did exactly that, and they created huge immigrant communities in cities like Boston and New York.

Back home, the British government's response to the famine was mixed. Many parliamentarians excoriated their colleagues' lack of action and demanded that relief funds be sent to the starving Irish peasants. But others, including many landlords within Ireland, profited from the sharp rise in food prices and did nothing to help their starving workers. Because of this malicious exploitation on the part of some English landlords and the British government's complacency, some Irish people have gone as far as to claim that the famine was not only a natural disaster, but also an act of indirect genocide. Whether or not that claim is accurate, it was at the very least one of the most deadly famines in the history of modern Europe.

Killarney

You can walk from one end of Killarney to the other in about 40 minutes. But packed into that tiny space is a huge selection of Ireland's liveliest pubs, and the surrounding countryside includes some extremely beautiful scenery, wildlife, and picturesque castles. Between its 19th-century architecture and the timeless atmosphere of its storefronts and bars, Killarney can feel like a slice of a bygone era in Irish history. (This is, in part due to a recent ban on plastic store signs – half a protection for the town's scenic charm, and half a way of protecting the traditional signmaking craft.)

Eat, Sleep, and Drink

Tiny Killarney (population 14,219) has only a small number of hotels, restaurants, and pubs, but all of them are excellent. You'd have to go out of your way to have a bad experience here.

Since the town is so small and easy to walk, it doesn't matter much where you stay – the choice is really dependent on personal preference. The top end of the spectrum is **Aghadoe Heights Hotel & Spa**, a 5-star establishment with spectacular views, fine dining, and plenty of pampering. At the budget end, you'll find **Neptune's Hostel**, where backpackers come not only for the cheap rooms but also the many day tours operated by the hostel's management. There's also the charming **Sugan Hostel** downtown, a Mom & Pop operation whose owners love to socialize with travelers. In between, there are plenty of small B&B's (including the luxury guesthouse at **Inveraray Farm**) and mid-range hotels.

Battlements of Ross Castle
(photo credit: Eire Sarah via Creative Commons)

For meals, the most traditional option is probably **The Laurels** on High Street. It's a combination pub/restaurant, so it may get a little crowded in the late evenings, but for a lunch or dinner it's got some of the best food in Killarney. There's also **Treyvaud's** right across the street, which isn't on most tourists' radar screen, but serves an eclectic selection of high-quality international fare. After dinner, if you're looking for a place to drink, try just walking up and down High Street and the adjacent New Street. These two thoroughfares have the majority of the town's pubs, and most are fairly small traditional pubs. The one nightclub in Killarney is **The Grand** on Main Street, which combines a live music venue ("The Bar") with a disco dance hall ("The Club").

Killarney National Park

Killarney sits right on the edge of Killarney National Park, a small but exquisitely beautiful space of winding trails and waterfalls, roughly 8 miles from end to end. There are several world-class day hikes within the park, as well as lots of trails for cycling. At the edge of the park is **Ross Castle**, an especially scenic ruin that affords spectacular views of the town and the park beyond.

Killarney National Park
(photo credit: Eire Sarah via Creative Commons)

Local Sports

Fitzgerald Stadium is home to several of the teams representing County Kerry in the inter-county Irish leagues. The stadium is fairly intimate, so it's a great way to see local sports heroes battle with visitors from the neighboring counties. If Kerry is going up against Cork in a Gaelic Football match, it will seem like the whole county has congregated in Fitzgerald stadium – this is one of the most storied sports rivalries in Munster.

Innisfallen and Lough Leane

Lough Leane is a huge, tranquil lake that takes up much of the National Park. Guided boat trips leave regularly from **Ross Castle** to take in the sights of the lake, especially the mysterious island of Innisfree, whose scenic shoreline and ruined monastery have inspired generations of poets and travelers. If you're more interested in traveling independently, you can always rent a canoe or kayak in town and paddle out to the island yourself.

The Ring of Kerry

Ireland's highest mountains are located on **Iveragh Peninsula**, the wide spit of land jutting out to the west of Kilarney. This spectacular peninsula is circled by the **Ring of Kerry**, a stretch of highway roughly 100 miles long. You could fill an entire guidebook with all the historic, geological, and cultural wonders that line this highway, but here are just a few of the key locations to consider:

(photo credit: High Contrast via Wikimedia Commons)

Carrauntoohil

Cahergall Ringfort, Interior
(photo credit: Theboykenny via Wikimedia Commons)

Though set several miles back from the highway, **Ireland's tallest mountain** is visible from the road for much of the eastern portion of the Ring of Kerry. There are several trails on the mountain, but it's best to go with a guide if you plan to make an attempt on the summit. At 3,406 feet, it's hardly daunting for an experienced mountaineer, but remember that every one of those feet is rising almost directly from sea level! The ridges are extremely steep and sharp-sided, and can be treacherous for the inexperienced mountaineer.

Prehistoric Sites

Because of the sparse population and lack of large cities, this region has some of the best-preserved prehistoric sites in all of Ireland. The Ring of Kerry is thick with standing stones, ringforts, and other Stone Age constructions, many of which are easily accessible from the highway. Perhaps the most striking is **Cahergall Ringfort** on the western edge of the peninsula. This fort, thought to be about 2,000 years old, has been carefully reconstructed by archaeologists, so visitors can see what it would have looked like when it was new. For those more interested in the romance of untouched ruins, the slightly younger **Staigue Fort** is unreconstructed and can be seen in its natural state.

The Skelligs

Off the edge of Iveragh Peninsula are the tiny sea-battered rocks known as **Little Skellig** and **Skellig Michael**. Centuries ago, Skellig Michael housed a small monastery where early Irish Christians sought utter isolation from the material world. Their dwellings, still preserved on the island, are listed as a UNESCO World Heritage Site. Standing amid these simple stone huts, it's baffling to think that human beings lived their whole lives on this tiny outcrop amid the waves. There's a **visitor's center** on nearby Valentia Island that gives an excellent overview of the site's history and how the monks managed to survive on this seemingly barren land.

Little Skellig, from the Monastery
(photo credit: Russavia via Wikimedia Commons)

Little Skellig has never had a human settlement, and very few humans have ever set foot on its steep-sided shores. However, the total lack of predators has made this island a perfect haven for thousands and thousands of gannets. These large, majestic birds make their nests right on the exposed cliff-faces, and the sound they produce, as it echoes off the jagged rocks, creates an absolutely otherworldly sensation. The island is closed to the public due to environmental and safety concerns, but it's relatively easy to get boat tours that go right up alongside the rocks to give visitors a glimpse of the vast bird colony.

The Dingle Peninsula

One of the great bastions of traditional Irish culture is the western portion of County Kerry. This region is home to some of Ireland's great wilderness areas, and has produced some of the island's best musicians, poets, and storytellers. The Dingle Peninsula, in particular, is an outstanding destination for culture, *craic*, and undisturbed nature.

(Photo by the author)

Getting In & Getting Around

This remote region of Ireland is a little complicated to get to. Trains only run as far as **Tralee** at the base of the peninsula, and from there on you'll either have to take buses, taxis, or your own two feet. Fortunately, the bus trip is spectacularly scenic, passing through the **Conor Pass** on its way into **Dingle Town**. Once you get into the Peninsula, your options for public transportation are quite limited, and your best bet is probably to get the phone number of a reliable local taxi driver – ask for recommendations at your hotel or hostel.

One of the best ways to get around the peninsula is on foot. A stunning set of footpaths, collectively known as the **Dingle Way**, will lead you from Tralee through Dingle Town, out to the end of the peninsula and then back again, along the way taking in all the best mountain views and prehistoric sites. The trails total just over 75 miles of shining coastlines, towering mountains, sheer seaside cliffs, and a huge proliferation of historic sites and monuments. An adventurous traveler with a quick step can cover the whole thing in the space of about a week. This, tied with the Ring of Kerry, is easily the best long-term trek that Ireland has to offer.

Tralee

Outside the Author's Home in Dingle
(photo by the author)

Any trip to the Dingle Peninsula will likely take you through **Tralee**, a mid-sized town of 23,000 that is the main transportation hub in this part of Ireland. Tralee has a few decent hotels and at least one reputable hostel, but other than that there's not much to see – it's just a jumping-off point for the rest of the peninsula.

Dingle Town

Dingle (also known as *An Daingean* in Irish) is the musical capital of West Kerry. It's a rustic town of just over 2,000 res-idents, roughly a mile and a half from end to end, with a stunning profusion of tiny pubs. Dingle is said to have about **50 pubs** within the city limits, including a small nightclub on the outskirts of town, where local students congregate on weekend evenings. The best place for local music is undoubtedly *An Droichead Beag*, affectionately known as the *Droichead* (DRO-head) or simply the Small Bridge. In this large, centrally-located bar you'll hear a spectacular session of traditional music each evening, and around midnight it seems that the whole town has packed in under the exposed rafters to hear the musicians ply their trade.

Fungie Says "Hello"
(photo credit: Duloup via Wikimedia Commons)

Dingle is popular enough with tourists that there are several places to stay, including the historic **Dingle Bay Hotel**. The vast majority of travelers, however, choose to stay either in a B&B or any of the handful of youth hostels scattered around the town. Restaurants are somewhat harder to find, although many of the pubs have kitchens. The **Dingle Pub** has particularly excellent food, and there are a number of seafood restaurants along the harbor.

Dingle is also the home of **Fungie**, a friendly dolphin who has lived in the Dingle Bay for at least 30 years. For reasons no one can quite explain, Fungie loves to follow boats in and out of the harbor, so it's very easy to see him when the weather is good. The most intimate way to visit Fun-gie, though, is to rent a kayak and paddle out to the middle of the bay on a clear, sunny afternoon. This inscrutable dolphin is almost guaranteed to pop up for a visit if you're patient.

Abandoned Village on the Great Blasket
(photo by the author)

Along the road from Tralee to Dingle, you'll go through the **Conor Pass**, a stunningly wild mountain valley that lights up in stunning green from April to September. There are very few trails in this area, but it's unbeatable for wilderness hiking. For a slightly more challenging hike, head for **Brandon Mountain** on the northern side of the peninsula. This mountain, held sacred by the ancient Celts, is the tallest in the region and offers some spectacularly dramatic vistas.

The Blasket Islands

At the very western end of the Dingle Peninsula, beyond the cliffs of Slea Head, are the abandoned islands known as the Blaskets. The **Great Blasket Island** was once home to a proud community of Irish-speaking farmers who produced some of the best literature ever written in Irish. Economic hardship forced the villagers to abandon their island in 1953, and today it is home only to roving bands of feral sheep. But it is a spectacularly scenic place, and the rolling hills of the Great Blasket Island offer glorious views of the surrounding waves. The **Blasket Center**, located in the mainland village of Dunquin, gives an excellent introduction to the islands' history and culture.

Part V
Ulster (The North)

Proud. Fierce. Independent. Ulster has been set apart from the rest of Ireland since ancient times, when the warriors of this northern kingdom proved themselves on the battlefield and became some of the most feared on the island. Today, the ancient kingdom is split in two by the line of partition separating the Republic of Ireland from Northern Ireland. When Ireland launched its War of Independence against Great Britain (see p. 18), Protestant Unionists in the North refused to join in, preferring to remain as part of the United Kingdom. This communal split has affected the history of Ulster ever since, and there's no mistaking it when you visit the major cities of the North.

But, despite its reputation for violence, Ulster has much to offer the traveler – **Belfast** is a large, cosmopolitan city much like many others in the United Kingdom, and the northern **coast** has some of the most dramatic geological formations in Ireland. And as the wounds of the war begin to heal, Northern Ireland is blossoming into a stable, peaceful community.

(Image Courtesy of Wikimedia Commons)

Mural Marking Unionist Territory in East Belfast
(Photo credit: Keith Ruffles via Wikimedia Commons)

Spend just a few hours walking around Belfast, and you'll see some striking murals painted all over the walls of the town. Many commemorate fallen neighbors, battles, or black-masked militias pointing submachine guns out at the viewer. Even without any knowledge of the history of Nor-thern Ireland, there's no mistaking the message: this city was once a battleground, and the scars of communal conflict are still pain-fully visible.

The violence in Northern Ireland (known as "The Troubles") had its early stages in the beginnings of the Irish War of Independence, starting around 1914. When English-speaking Protestants realized that their Irish-speaking Catholic neighbors were planning to rise up against the British government, they formed counter-militias to oppose the revolution. With the end of the war in 1920, the island was split into an independent Republic of Ireland and a country of Northern Ireland that would remain part of the U.K.

Naturally, this outcome was condemned by Nationalists in the north, who had struggled to create a unified republic in their homeland and were now going to be separated from their fellow Irishmen in the southern counties. But they were in the minority, and the Protestant majority was firm in its resolve to remain under the London government.

In the 1960s, increasing tension between the two communities led to an outbreak of violence, which in turn sparked a series of reprisal bombings, assassinations, and pitched street battles between Nationalists and Unionists. Thousands were killed in the decades of violence, and Northern Ireland developed a reputation as a warzone. Tourists stayed away, concerned that they would fall victim to a car bomb or a gun battle in the streets.

The violence finally began to ebb in 1998, with the signing of the Good Friday Agreement. This complex accord helped to settle many of the issues left unresolved by the partition of 1920, and met the agreement of militants on both sides of the conflict.

Northern Ireland is still a place of communal tension, as the murals clearly show. But the agreement demonstrates that both sides are willing to make the sacrifices and concessions necessary to bring an end to the decades of violence that have wracked Northern Ireland.

Belfast

Well, in a neat little town they call Belfast, apprenticed to trade I was bound. Many an hour's sweet happiness have I spent in that neat little town!

Belfast City Hall
(Photo by the author)

Northern Ireland's bustling capital city is hardly a "neat little town" anymore – it's a thriving and diverse metropolis with a pop-ulation of more than a quarter-million. And despite decades of politically motivated vio-lence, it was recently declared to be the **safest city in the UK** based on crime figures per capita.

Planes

Belfast is served by two airports. **George Best Belfast City Airport** is smaller and nearer to the city center, but has very few international flights – it mostly serves flights from elsewhere in the U.K. and France.

Belfast International Airport is larger and significantly further away from town, but it takes direct flights from all over the world. You can get into central Belfast via a regular bus service (roughly 45 minutes, depending on traffic), or by taking a cab, which should cost about £25.

Trains

Trains run between Belfast and Dublin several times each day (a journey of about two and a half hours), other than that the trains in Northern Ireland mainly go to industrial cities and not major tourist destinations. The main station is **Belfast Central Train Station** along the River Lagan and just a couple of miles southwest of the harbor.

Buses and Ferries

The bus/ferry combination is one of the best ways to reach Belfast from other UK cities such as Glasgow and Edinburgh. The bus drives straight onto the ferry, which then docks in the harbor. There are also plenty of municipal busses within Northern Ireland which have broader coverage than the trains. Northern Ireland is compact enough that **tour buses** can take you pretty easily to any of the major destinations in the area.

Car Rental

In most of Ireland, it's not a great idea to rent a car because of the low quality roads and erratic behavior of other drivers. In Northern Ireland, however, the roads tend to be more reliable and the drivers are less unpredictable. If you do plan to rent a car, though, make sure you're comfortable driving on the left!

Getting Around in Belfast

Although Belfast is less compact than other cities on the island, its key sights are mostly within walking distance of the central Train Station. However, there's a lot to see here, and unless your budget is very tight it's usually worthwhile to invest in a **Hop-on Hop-off Bus** ticket. For just £10-15, you get freedom of movement around the city, plus an expert tour guide who can explain each location in detail – this is especially valuable in a destination like Belfast, where the shadow of history is long and nearly everything around you requires some interpretation.

Where to Stay

Belfast has a full range of accommodations, but they tend to cluster around the lower end of the budget spectrum. The hostels here are some of the best you'll find anywhere, especially the **City Backpacker** in the southern portion of the city center. The cheapest option is probably a bed in one of the multiple-occupancy dorms at **Arnie's Backpackers**, which will run somewhere around £10 per night.

Because of the history of violence, Belfast hasn't attracted a lot of high-end tourists, so it doesn't have many luxury hotels. The best option for travelers looking to splurge is probably the **Merchant Hotel**, which opened less than 10 years ago and so hasn't yet built up its reputation. But early reports say that it's extremely comfortable, and it's certainly a spectacular specimen of architecture.

In between the hostels and the grand hotels, there are dozens of mid-range options, B&B's, and international hotels chains of fairly predictable quality. The **Ramada Encore** is the most centrally-located, while the **Ibis Belfast** is quite inexpensive and located in the very pleasant neighborhood around the Botanical Gardens.

Eating in Belfast

The dining options in Belfast are extremely diverse, although it's not always easy to find a traditional Irish meal here. You're covered on Indian, Mexican, Thai, and Chinese at all budget levels, but it takes a little work to find the sort of food that's more commonplace in Munster or Connacht. Here are a few local favorites for traditional meals:

Bright's Restaurant (41-43 Castle Street and 23-25 High Street)

Locals will swear by one location or the other, but most travelers report that they're pretty similar. There's no other place in Belfast to get traditional food this cheap, especially on their spectacular breakfast menu.

Darcy's Restaurant (10 Bradbury Place)

A step above Bright's in terms of price and atmosphere, but still pretty inexpensive. This is a great family restaurant, especially if you can take advantage of their early bird specials, which are quite cheap, but end at 7pm. Perfect destination for an early dinner!

Restaurant Michael Deane (36-40 Howard St)

Creative takes on Irish and international cuisine. Belfast's only restaurant with a Michelin star, and with all the atmosphere and service to boot. This place is definitely not cheap.

Pubs & Clubs

After Dublin, Belfast has some of the most notorious nightlife on the island. Young tourists often join local students for the **Belfast Pub Crawl**, which lasts all night and costs a very reasonable £8.

Don't talk politics in a Belfast pub. The city is still culturally segregated into Catholic/Republican and Protestant/Unionist neighborhoods, and bars have always been particularly subject to that distinction. You probably won't know which type of bar you're in, and either way it's just better to avoid the potentially explosive topic of partition and The Troubles.

Traditional Pubs

McHugh's Bar & Restaurant (29-31 Queens Square)

McHugh's is housed in the oldest building in Belfast (though, at just over 300 years old, it's still a baby compared to many buildings in Dublin or Cork). This relatively large pub provides an excellent entertainment venue and serves a diverse clientele of students, locals, and tourists.

The Kitchen Bar (36-40 Victoria Square)

Renowned for having some of the best atmosphere in Belfast, the Kitchen Bar also (as its name suggests) serves excellent food all through the night. Many bars in Belfast will feel more like Scottish or English pubs than Irish ones, but the Kitchen is a notable exception.

Ryan's Bar and Restaurant (116-118 Lisburn Road)

Best boxties in Belfast, hands down. Also a great beer selection and charming atmosphere.

Kelly's Cellars
(Photo credit: Albert Bridge via Wikimedia Commons)

Kelly's Cellars (30-32 Bank Street)

Kelly's has traditional music on the weekends, and its hidden-away lo-cation means that you'll see pretty small crowds and very few tourists. During the 1798 uprising against the British, Kelly's was an important safehouse for Republican Nationalists of the United Irishmen. Kelly's is a little tough to find, so you may have to ask someone for directions – it's tucked away in a little white building just off Castle Street, and the signage out front is subtle.

White's Tavern (2-4 Winecellar Entry)

The typical European nightclub is not as popular in Belfast as it is in Dublin or even Cork, but the closest thing is probably White's tavern, which has a Friday night disco and live bands on most weekend nights. With two distinct levels playing different styles of music, the bar is usually pretty packed on the weekends.

Limelight (17 Ormeau Avenue)

Part of a trio of popular clubs that cater to the alternative/indie crowd. (The other two, located right next door, are **Katy Daly's** and the **Spring & Airbrake**.) Several live gigs per week, often from internationally known touring artists. Particularly popular on Tuesday nights.

The Parador (116-118 Ormeau Rd)

Excellent jazz club with cocktails and a pleasant atmosphere. The live jazz happens on Thursday nights, and the bar also offers a trivia game on Wednesday nights.

Key Sights in Belfast

Belfast City Hall

The City Hall is one of the most striking buildings in the city, and its magnificent green dome is a perfect encapsulation of turn-of-the-century British architecture. The best way to see City Hall may be from the huge Ferris wheel next door, which gives spectacular views of the city and the surrounding countryside.

Titanic Quarter

In the late 19th century, Belfast was one of the most important shipbuilding ports in the United Kingdom, and the culmination of its industrial might was supposed to be the construction of the world's first unsinkable ship – the Titanic. That star-crossed vessel was built right in Belfast Harbor, and there are plenty of tour guides who will take you around the drydocks and explain how the ship was constructed. You can also visit on your own, but the harbor looks pretty nondescript if you don't have someone around to explain its details.

Palm House, Belfast Botanic Gardens
(Photo credit: Man Vyi via Wikimedia Commons)

Botanic Gardens

Widely considered to be one of the most beautiful formal gardens in the world, the Belfast Botanic Gardens occupy a large green swath about 2 miles south of the city center. Its exterior gardens are sublimely designed with winding paths and a bewildering variety of plant life. It's the in-terior gardens of the **Palm House**, though, that attract the most visitors. The house is climate controlled at all seasons, allowing visitors to enjoy tropical plants that would otherwise never survive here.

Ulster Museum

Right on the edge of the Botanic Gardens is the Ulster Museum, a **free** museum covering history, archaeology, art, and natural history all under one roof. It's a must-see for anyone interested in learning about Ulster. It has an especially compelling visit on The Troubles, which covers the conflict in a balanced and compassionate way, with the focus on the human experience of communal violence rather than on any one political perspective.

Political Murals

Nationalist Mural
(Photo credit: Man Vyi via Wikimedia Commons)

They can be extremely intense and often a little unsettling, but the murals around Belfast are an authentic expression of what it feels like to grow up in a warzone, and they express the city's history better than any book or documentary. The majority of murals are located around Falls Road and Shankill Road, but they're scattered around the city. Getting a **Mural Tour** is definitely recommended, as this is the best way to understand the many stories being depicted in these remarkable works of art.

Belfast Castle

Though technically not a castle, this regal home is a great way to see the city on a clear day. It's located on a hill about four miles north of the city. The view from its top floors is truly spectacular, and takes in miles of coastline along with the city itself and the rolling hills all around.

Giant's Causeway and Airds Snout
(Photo credit: Pam Fray via Creative Commons)

Giant's Causeway

Northern Ireland's coastline is famous for its scenic hills and gentle waves, but there's one spot that eclipses all the rest in fame. The unique hexagonal columns of the Giant's Cause-way in **County Antrim** attract thousands of visitors each year and are considered one of the greatest natural treasures of the United Kingdom. They are also one of the natural wonders on the list of UNESCO World Her-itage Sites. Located about **40 miles north of Belfast**, the Causeway is easily reachable by buses and day tours.

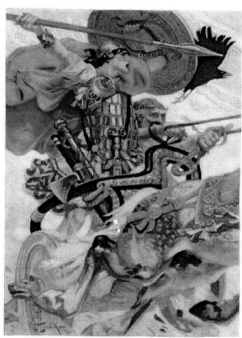

Cuchulainn Rides into Battle
(Painting by Joseph Christian Leyendecker, public domain)

Long before partition, before the British Empire – even before the Romans ever set foot on the British Isles – Ulster was a flourishing civilization and the most powerful kingdom on the island. And it was this culture that produced Ireland's most storied warrior, and perhaps the most beloved hero in all of Irish mythology: **Cuchulainn.**

Cuchulainn (koo-HULL-ann) was a young boy in the fortress town of Emuin Macha. As a child, he was frail and shy, and the other boys rejected him from their number. But Cuchulainn was no ordinary child – he was the grandson of the Celtic God of Light, and he would not be bullied for long. One day, when one of the boys was pushing him around to the jeers of a few friends, Cuchulainn's temper broke and he suddenly transformed into a terrifying monster with sharp teeth, a long snapping tongue, and claws on the ends of his fingers.

From that day forward, Cuchulainn was blessed (or cursed) with "warp-spasms" – every time rage or battle-fury came over him, his body would transform and he would become a fearsome beast. After winning many duels, he became known as the "Hound of Ulster," and the king rewarded his prowess with a place of honor at the high table.

This great warrior not only defended the king's court — he also charged into the field of battle alone when Ulster's enemies were on the march, and singlehandedly defended his homeland against the armies of Connacht under **Queen Medb** (see p. 39) But although his spectacular defense was successful, Cu-chulainn would not survive the final battle. Dealt his death wound, Cuchulainn resolved to die on his feet, and lashed himself to an ancient standing stone.

That stone still stands today, hidden away in the corner of a backcountry field in County Louth. The stone is marked only by a tiny plaque near the road, but fans of Irish mythology can often be seen placing their hands on the stone's broad face, trying to find any traces that the Hound of Ulster might have left behind.

Though not part of Northern Ireland, Donegal is still one of the counties of Ulster. And its location, almost entirely cut off from the rest of the Republic, means that it sees very few tourists. Donegal is not easy to get to, and not used to large numbers of tourists, but it's one of the most beautiful parts of the island, and still a relatively undiscovered gem of hiking, coastlines, and Celtic culture.

(photo credit: NUIGMC via Wikimedia Commons)

Towns

The most populous town in this sparsely populated countryside is **Letterkenny** (pop. 18,000) at the mouth of the River Swilly. It's something of a student town and has easily the best shopping and nightlife in Donegal. It's also just 10 miles or so from the National Park, making it a decent base of operations for hikers. There are also a couple of clubs in **Glentiles**, but frankly if it's the mix-and-mingle experience you're looking for, Donegal is probably the wrong destination.

Those interested in surfing and water sports should head for the village of **Bundoran** on the shores of Donegal Bay. In addition to a sandy beach (a rarity for Ireland), it also has excellent golf facilities and plenty of Gaelic Games. There's also the tiny seaside town of **Dunfanaghy** (pop. 312), which has a huge, usually quite empty, sandy beachfront. There's only one hotel in town, and it's a bit rustic, but the location is hard to beat when it comes to waves and open water. No nightlife to speak of.

There's no better reason to come to Donegal than hiking, however, and for that you have to get outside the "major" population centers.

Hiking and Walking

Donegal is a rugged landscape with a variety of seaside cliffs, sharp mountain ridges, and rolling hills. Much of the land is uncultivated, and you'll be amazed at the sense of wilderness and isolation that you can achieve with even a short trek outside the towns.

Mount Errigal
(Photo credit: Owen Doody via Creative Commons)

Much of the hiking is concentrated in **Glenveagh National Park**, in the inland reaches of northern Donegal. The park's mountains are not easy to climb, and it's best to make sure that someone at your hotel (or the visitor's center) knows where you're going and when you're expected to return. There's also the spectacular **Glenveagh Castle**, whose architecture is nearly as grand as the mountains themselves. Admission to the castle is relatively cheap (€5 for adults), and the grounds are extremely tranquil and pleasant.

Just outside the park, but visible from within, is **Mount Errigal**, the tallest mountain in Donegal. Although it hardly rivals the mountains of County Kerry in terms of outright size (it's only 2,464 feet high), its incredible shape and the steepness of its snow-covered slopes make for an invigorating climb.

Climbing the mountain in winter can be slightly treacherous, but it's still possible. In addition, like so much of Donegal, the mountain almost devoid of tourists.

In most places, the coast of Donegal is no less dramatic than its interior. The county is ringed by stunning coastal cliffs, of which the most famous are located at **Slieve League** in the far west of the county. In addition to the cliffs themselves, the site has crafts and artisinal foods that are worth the visit on their own.

Part VI: No One Leaves Ireland for Long

(photo by the author)

I was standing on the ridge of Croachskearda, just south of the Conor Pass and a few miles from my home in Dingle. It was late winter, the mountain streams were just beginning to thaw, and the grass was still in its amber earth tones, having not yet bloomed into the verdure of spring. And as I looked down at the valley, idly counting the peaks and lakes in this one, tiny corner of the Irish wilderness, I realized that I would never meet them all. I would never climb all of those hills or dip my fingers in all those frigid pools of water, not even if I lived my whole life right there on the mountainside.

In Ireland, there's always another hill to climb.

There's always another magical glen to discover, another standing stone to marvel at. Another little village pub with its rich clamor of glasses and songs. There's always another tale to be woven.

That's what keeps people coming back to this incredible island – the more you get to know it, the more there is to explore. Its very soil teems with mystery, and yet every inch of ground feels somehow familiar, as if you've always been here. More quickly than you'd ever expect, it begins to feel like home.

So bear that in mind before you plan a trip to Ireland. You may leave the island, but it'll never fully leave you. And, sooner or later, you'll be drawn inexorably back to its green shores once again.

Enjoy your trip!

Dagny Taggart

>> Get Full Online Language Courses With Audio Lessons <<

Would you like to learn a new language before you start your trip? I think that's a great idea. Now, why don't you do it 300% *FASTER*?

I've partnered with the most revolutionary language teachers to bring you the very language online courses I've ever seen. It's a mind-blowing program specifically created for language hackers such as ourselves. It will allow you learn ANY language, from French to Chinese, 3x faster, straight from the comfort of your own home, office, or wherever you may be. It's like having an unfair advantage!

You can choose from a wide variety of languages, such as French, Spanish, Italian, German, Chinese, Portuguese, and A TON more.

Each Online Course consists of:

+ 91 Built-In Lessons
+ 33 Interactive Audio Lessons
+ 24/7 Support to Keep You Going

The program is extremely engaging, fun, and easy-going. You won't even notice you are learning a complex foreign language from scratch. And before you realize it, by the time you go through all the lessons you will officially become a truly solid speaker.

Old classrooms are a thing of the past. It's time for a revolution.

If you'd like to go the extra mile, then follow the link below, and let the revolution begin!

>> http://bitly.com/foreign-language-courses <<

CHECK OUT THE COURSE »

PS: Can I Ask You a Quick Favor?

If you liked the book, please leave a nice review on Amazon! I'd absolutely love to hear your feedback. Every time I read your reviews... you make me smile. I'd be immensely thankful if you go to Amazon now, and write down a quick line sharing with me your experience. I personally read ALL the reviews there, and I'm thrilled to hear your feedback and honest motivation. It's what keeps me going, and helps me improve everyday =)

<u>Please go Amazon now and drop a quick review sharing your experience!</u>

***

<u>THANKS!</u>

***

ONCE YOU'RE BACK,
FLIP THE PAGE!
BONUS CHAPTER AHEAD
=)

Introduction
Are You Ready for an Amazing Journey?

Welcome to England, a tiny island packed full of the extraordinary and the charming. Welcome to a country where no two experiences are the same. Gaze up at famous London landmarks then wander through deserted forest and rolling farmland. Spend an afternoon in an alternative working class suburb before enjoying an evening engrossed in Shakespeare. Discover the home of the Beatles and then discover the insides of a traditional English pub. England offers something for everyone, yet at its heart, is a very authentic and quintessential experience. Cream tea and scones, pork pies, flat caps, girls wearing short skirts in winter; the country stoically maintains its bizarre traditions and peculiar styles. No matter how much the scenery and accents change, an indelible imprint of Englishness follows you at every turn.

But what is England? Even the locals aren't so sure. Perhaps the country of quaint village greens and eating fish and chips along a pebbled beach. Maybe the chaotic buzz of the capital, or the trendy neighborhoods you'll find on its outskirts. Is it the Queen and the wonderful stately homes that dot the countryside? Manchester United, fried breakfasts, gothic cathedrals, Big Ben, cups of tea, more cups of tea, cobblestone streets of delight and intrigue; exploring England provides a continual immersion in both the famous and the unusual, the idiosyncratic and the popular. But the country's greatest appeal is its size. England is tiny and far smaller than most visitor's realize. Cramming a lot into a few days is relatively easy. First timers are quickly enchanted, while regular visitors always have something new to discover.

This guidebook has a very English approach at its heart. It's straightforward and to the point, providing the information you need to effectively plan and travel to the country. After all, when there is so much to discover and decipher, you need a guide that doesn't waffle or meander. Yet at the same time it likes to indulge in the eccentric, evoking authentic England and ensuring you seek out everything from your English experience. Think of it as a local holding your hand, guiding and revealing, but never demanding or forcing. Think of it as a fish and chip packet getting warm on your lap, sitting by a log fire in a country pub, or watching a musical in West End London. This guide is here to assist and support, but ensure England is always *your* experience.

This is a country that everyone has to visit at least once in a lifetime, but which way do you turn? For some it's following a single paradigm, recreating the famous scenes from movies or shows like Downtown Abbey. Others plan more geographically, connecting the country's excellent transport network and dipping into a dozen compellingly different destinations. There's the visitor who wants a rural scene; dry stone walls, countless sheep, and endless hiking trails. Then let's not forget the mad glory of central London. This guide covers it all, north to south, east to west, and every odd little part in between. Oh, and it's written by a local...you were looking for the real English experience right?

Let's get started!

Chapter 1
Welcome to the Mighty England!

Most visitors land in London, the huge capital city that has enough to keep people entertained for months. Central London is where you'll find the infamous monuments and sights; Big Ben, Buckingham Palace, red double decker buses passing by St Paul's Cathedral… It's tourist central but it's quite wonderful. London actually constitutes of a multitude of distinct neighborhoods. Head to East London for vibrant working class suburbs that have become very cool. Go west for upmarket shopping and luxuriant districts, north for glimpses of classic old London, and south for a mix of it all.

Within an easy day trip of London you'll discover Southeast England, a historic place of medieval towns, world heritage sites, and alternative cities. Oxford, Canterbury, Brighton; choose to base yourself in London or leave the capital and easily tour these unique attractions.

Head Southwest and the rolling green farmlands of England begin to dominate the scene. It's quite a journey, the rural land packed with quaint stone villages, Neolithic rocks, and the country's best beaches. It's serene and enigmatic, each stop dancing with color and intimacy.

The Midlands is England's forgotten land, a cultural melting pot that most people merely skip through on route to The North. What it lacks in famous attractions it makes up for in delightful national parks, literary history, and intriguing cities.

If Scotland had voted for independence from the UK then The North would have tried to do the same. It's where you'll find England at its quintessentially bizarre best; strange accents, funny traditions, post-industrial cities, and historic market towns. This is the home of English popular music, God's own country (Yorkshire), famous football teams, and huge swathes of picturesque national park. Yes, it rains a lot here, but it's worth it.

England Highlights

Before you go head first into this guide let's indulge in the variety that England can provide. Here are selections of both the iconic and indelibly unique experiences you can discover.

- Keep gasping in delight as you explore Central London and come face to face with all the classic scenes. Double decker buses, the Houses of Parliament, Tower Bridge, bright red phone boxes, Piccadilly Circus, then savor it all from the top of the London Eye. You won't meet many locals, but you'll fill the camera roll with dozens of famous sights. *(see Chapter 4: London)*

- Wander the cute medieval streets of Oxford, reveling in the illustrious history of this stunning university town. Once you're done admiring the buildings and cathedral, step inside atmospheric taverns and explore side-streets that dance with charm. *(see Chapter 5: Around London and Southeast England)*

- Go back in time and stand before the great Neolithic rocks of Stonehenge, an ancient riddle that historians are still struggling to solve. Nowhere can better exemplify the time travel conundrum of England, particularly if you've come straight from the city lights of London. *(see Chapter 6: Southwest England)*

- Get lost in the rolling hills of the Peak District National Park. Hike along deserted country trails and then reappear besides a cute traditional pub. For a remote escape into rural England it's hard to find a more fitting place. *(see Chapter 7: The Midlands)*

- Go on a musical tinged journey through Liverpool, feasting your eyes on the Victorian monuments before a *Magical Mystery Tour* reveals the hometown of the Beatles. Even at 2pm on a Wednesday you can be singing along in the atmospheric cavern where the fab four first performed. *(see Chapter 8: The North)*

Unique Experiences

- Get on the underground and alight in East London, full of once dingy neighborhoods that now burst with color, creativity, and England's modern multiculturalism. Wander down the Bangladeshi influenced Brick Lane, explore graffiti covered pop-up shops and markets, and discover where real Londoners go to hang out. *(see Chapter 4: London)*

- Dip your feet into the sand of Brighton beach and then experience the city's desire to promote alternative culture. It's hard to find a more entertaining night out than Brighton, then again, it's difficult to go ten minutes without spotting something funky or weird along the open promenade. *(see Chapter 5: Around London and Southeast England)*

- Indulge in the ancient splendor of Bath, a city that's a living UNESCO World Heritage site and a museum space of abbeys, arched bridges, glorious townhouses, and Roman baths. For artistic beauty, few cities in the world can match Bath's Georgian painting (see Chapter 6: Southwest England)

- Alight in Nottingham and feast your eyes on the juxtaposition of modern England. You'll find old cathedrals, glistening shopping centers, cobbled streets, and bustling city bars. It's all well off the tourist trail, just remember to say "eyup duck," the local slang for "hello." (see Chapter 7: The Midlands)

- Forgive the grey skies as you amble through the winding roads of the Lake District, exploring green valleys punctuated by too many sheep and some serene lakes. The landscape here is as English as a cup of tea, and it won't be long before you're chatting with the locals about the weather (see Chapter 8: The North)

The bucolic landscapes of the Lake District

This guide is split into three distinct sections. Each is designed to offer the most essential information to both plan and maximize your experience. England is a relatively easy country to travel in. The transport infrastructure is excellent, as is the choice of hotels and availability of tourist information offices. This guide offers the shortcuts and need to know, without polluting essential information with the unnecessary. It is designed with every type of visitor in mind, and covers common interests and destinations. At the same time, it places a heavy emphasis on helping visitors discover authentic England and sidestep overpriced overhyped attractions.

What you won't find in this guide is very detailed information on individual hotels, entry ticket prices, or establishment phone numbers. Instead, the general information is explained and you're directed to the best sources of information. For example, there are thirty or so small bed and breakfast hotels in the city of York. Almost every visitor will stay in one of these "B & B's" and they all essentially offer the same experience.

Chapter 2 provides all the information you require to plan your trip to England. It discusses classic travel routes and potential itineraries, when to go, how much it's going to cost, and basic travel requirements. Whole section are dedicated to getting around and cutting down costs. Public transport can cost 90% less if you book it in advance, so you need to know about it before you arrive in the country. You'll also find information on the best ways to travel between regions. This chapter also details the accommodation types and standard options for getting a good night's sleep.

Chapter 3 is about maximizing your experience and immersing yourself in English culture. Things like what to eat, what to drink, remembering your manners, and staying safe. Strange mannerisms and customs are what make England so great, so it's worth having an overview before you land on the fair isle.

Chapters 4 - 8 provide detailed information about each destination. These chapters are divided into five geographical regions. Every destination is presented in the same way. You'll be introduced to the place and the experiences on offer. This quick succinct style should provide enough information for you to make an informed decision about whether it's a place to consider for your itinerary. Then the guide provides practical information to make your visit a reality, including how to get there, travel essentials, and how to orientate yourself on arrival.

To Check out the Rest of "*England For Tourists*" go to Amazon and Look for it Right Now!

Are you ready to exceed your limits? Then pick a book from the one below and start learning yet another new language. I can't imagine anything more fun, fulfilling, and exciting!

If you'd like to see the entire list of language guides (there are a ton more!), go to:

>>http://www.amazon.com/Dagny-Taggart/e/B00K54K6CS/<<

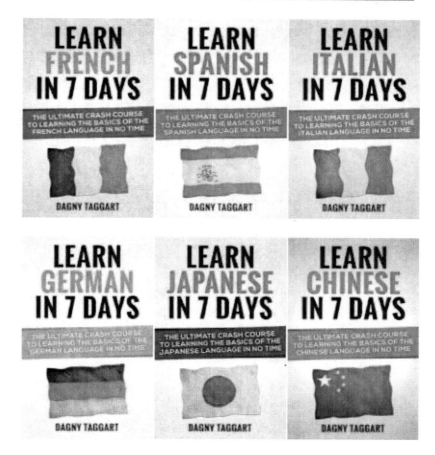

Dagny Taggart is a language enthusiast and polyglot who travels the world, inevitably picking up more and more languages along the way.

 Taggart's true passion became learning languages after she realized the incredible connections with people that it fostered. Now she just can't get enough of it. Although it's taken time, she has acquired vast knowledge on the best and fastest ways to learn languages. But the truth is, she is driven simply by her motive to build exceptional links and bonds with others.

She is inspired everyday by the individuals she meets across the globe. For her, there's simply not anything as rewarding as practicing languages with others because she gets to make friends with people from all that come from a variety of cultures. This, in turn, has broadened her mind and thinking more than she would have ever imagined it could.

Of course, as a result of her constant travels, Taggart has become an expert on planning trips and making the most of time spent out of what she calls her "base" town. She jokes that she's practically at the nomad status now, but she's more content to live that way.

She knows how to live on a manageable budget weather she's in Paris or Phnom Penh. She knows how to seek out the adventures and thrills, no doubt, lying in wait at any city she visits. She knows that reflection on each every experience is significant if she wants to grow as a traveler and student of the world's cultures.

Because of this, Taggart chooses to share her understanding of languages and travel so that others, too, can experience the same life-altering benefits she has.

CPSIA information can be obtained at www.ICGtesting.com
Printed in the USA
LVOW09s1623290615

444296LV00007B/232/P

9 781507 820582